Prospects f

£2.25

Fair Shares

Prospects for Tomorrow

Fair Shares

Ethics and the Global Economy

Timothy Gorringe

British Library Cataloguing-in-Publication Data
A catalogue record for this book is available from the British Library

ISBN 0-500-28115-7

Printed and bound in Slovenia by Mladinska Knjiga

CONTENTS

Karl Polanyi calls Aristotle 'a genius of common sense'. Part of that common sense (which notoriously did not extend to his perceptions of women or slaves) was to understand that economics is a subdiscipline of ethics – the question of the meaning and value of life. In particular Aristotle understood that economics was the outworking of a very fundamental virtue, justice, and that without justice the human community collapsed.

Adam Smith, the founder of modern economics, wrote within a sturdy common-sense tradition, but fatally divorced his two great treatises *The Theory of Moral Sentiments* (1759) and *The Wealth of Nations* (1776). When he writes about justice he has in mind criminal justice and the protection of property: the wider questions of what the medieval writers called 'distributive' justice, and what we call 'fair shares for all', simply did not occur to him. For Aristotle the connection of justice, ethics and economics was common sense, but this perspective has been largely lost sight of, except for a few discounted interlopers like John Ruskin and Frederick Soddy. When professional economists have insisted on this dimension in their work, they have too often been marginalized.

I am a theologian, and only as a theologian an ethicist, but I agreed to Yorick Blumenfeld's kind invitation to write this small book because I believe that economics is fundamentally a matter of common sense and therefore of ethics. This is not to deny its proper role as a scientific discipline, a role evidenced by my total dependence on the work of professional economists. I gladly acknowledge my debts to Herman Daly, Richard Douthwaite, David Korten, the staff of the Worldwatch Institute, of Oxfam and many others. In particular I have to thank the editorial team of *Prospects for Tomorrow*, Andy and Judi Newman, and especially Hugo Gorringe for a great many helpful criticisms and suggestions.

It is a great pleasure to record thanks to Herman Daly for both the highly stimulating theological reflections in his most recent book, but more still for pegging away at the economic common sense of finite and infinite for so long under the fire of so many of his economics peers. When his arguments are rejected by the orthodox (who uphold the neoclassical tradition and the necessity of growth, compound interest and incentives) as 'not the right way to look at things', I am reminded of Galileo's confrontation with the Inquisition: Aristotle said nothing about Jupiter having satellites – therefore they cannot exist.

I take comfort from the fact that the paradigm shift that Daly represents cannot be far off becoming the norm. Whether this will be soon enough to save the planet from the greed and hubris which so grievously threaten it remains to be seen.

CHAPTER 1

THE ECLIPSE OF SOCIAL JUSTICE?

> Justice is turned back,
> and righteousness stands at a distance . . .
> truth stumbles in the public square
>
> *Isaiah of Jerusalem*, eighth century BC

The Knowledge of Good and Evil

'No!' One of the first words a child learns. Or alternatively: 'Good girl!' or 'Well done!' When we go on to explain to the child why we praise or blame, we are outlining the fundamentals of ethics. 'What we call morality', writes Lewis Mumford, 'began in the mores, the life-conserving customs of the village.' (*The City in History*, 1961.) We, as humans, are fundamentally concerned with what is life-conserving. It is a question of what it is that promotes human well-being, what it is that makes for joy, creativity, security, the flourishing of love and happiness, and the exercise of the amazing talents of human beings. Whatever promotes all these things is 'good'; whatever destroys them is 'bad'. Therein lie our ethics, our morality, and the foundation of what we call social justice.

Human cultures are vast repositories of knowledge and wisdom gained by trial and error (though also of ancient hatreds and ossified spiritualities which can trap whole cultures in darkness). Ethical systems are the record of what it is that has been found to promote life and contain warnings about what destroys it. Every culture is made up of a tissue of traditions about what promotes or destroys life – traditions embodied in folk wisdom, sayings, proverbs, jokes, songs, children's stories, in practices of work and more formally in religion, in philosophy, in law – which constitute the fabric of daily life for a community. Doubtless, long before the invention of writing, human beings had discovered that being 'good' (promoting and conserving life) was not like falling off a log, nor just a matter of 'doing what comes naturally'. Some of the very earliest texts we have are law codes, prohibiting behaviour damaging to community life. The need for law, and for the formulation of codes of right and wrong, makes the point that for human beings 'nature' is in fact 'culture' – a matter of learning and training. We have to learn to use what Aristotle called our 'practical reason' (*phronesis*) just as we have to learn to use a saw and a plane, or a musical instrument, and we do this through our community, through the mediation of stories and traditions which teach us what practical reasoning and the nature of the good life are.

To take a rather more recent example, think of that passionate and profound essay on the good life, George Eliot's *Middlemarch* (1872). The down-to-earth Mary Garth, the daughter of an honest but impoverished builder and surveyor, is the foil to the intellectual heroine Dorothea Brooke. Mary and her father are the moral heart of the novel, representing a practical goodness quite unmoved by wealth, the urge for success or social or intellectual pretension. Their moral sense has been nurtured over centuries by a tradition in which 'the prince of darkness is a bad workman'. This is not exactly the work ethic. It is more a case that virtue is nourished by traditions of integrity, care, skill and attention which inform the whole of a particular understanding of life, which determine relationships as well as work and one's attitude to money. It leads, for example, as one would expect from George Eliot (Mary Ann Evans), who defied Victorian convention by living outside marriage with G.H. Lewes, to an understanding of marriage which only superficially resembles the bourgeois view. For her, marriage is the vocation of any new St Theresa, a hidden life through which 'the growing good of the world' is incalculably improved.

George Eliot has asked herself what on earth can be done about the savage capitalism of the 1860s and has replied that it can be tackled in and through the domestic relationships in which we are all in some way or other involved. Through marriage, she tells us, those things which make for life, the virtues, are nurtured within the wider community.

A New Dark Ages?

When George Eliot was writing it was widely assumed that human progress could be taken for granted, and many felt this was as true for ethics as for engineering. The course of the twentieth century has made us incalculably more sceptical.

In *After Virtue* (1981), one of the most celebrated works of moral philosophy of recent times, Alastair MacIntyre recalls the most famous historical example of widespread cultural collapse, the period the corporate memory of Europe for fifteen hundred years has known as the 'Dark Ages'. This was the period when wave upon wave of invasion – Goths, Vandals, Alans, Franks, Lombards, Saxons, Vikings – all but ruptured the continuity of Europe with the classical world. 'Artistic taste . . . underwent a regression, and so did morals . . . not only did the old stock of peasant superstitions re-emerge, but all the sexual perversions ran riot and acts of violence turned nastier.' (Le Goff, *Medieval Civilization*, 1988.) To this day we speak of wanton attacks on property as 'vandalism', and the propaganda of the First World War felt it sufficient to depict the Germans as 'the Hun'.

A key sign of the cultural collapse of our own day, according to MacIntyre, is what he calls 'emotivism', the inability of Western societies to agree about what counts as moral, the 'it seems to me' with which we preface every moral opinion. In his view it marks a similar rupture to that brought about by the first Dark Ages, for Western society no longer shares any common understanding of the good.

MacIntyre does not point to the obvious barbarities of the present century as evidence for the 'new Dark Ages', but one could be forgiven for doing so. We only have to recall the Armenian, Cambodian and Rwandan genocides, the Holocaust, the napalming of Vietnam, ethnic cleansing in the Balkans, the death squads whose work still goes on in Latin America, and the current death of 35,000 children each day from malnutrition and preventable disease. Huns and Vandals would have been hard put to create so dismal a record. No wonder that Edvard Munch's *The Scream*, painted in 1895, seems to many a Cassandra-like prophecy of the twentieth century. We of all people have learned the hard way of the fragility of goodness, the fact that the gains of culture and civilization are hard won and easily lost, and never to be taken for granted. The primary lesson of the Holocaust, says Peter Haas, is the susceptibility of human beings to new forms of moral discourse (*Morality after Auschwitz*, 1988). Far from people being endowed with an innate sense of right and wrong, as it was possible to believe in the self-confidence of the eighteenth century, morality seems to be a wax nose which can be moulded at will.

The Dark Ages of moral chaos supervene on a period when there are strong, if not unchallenged, traditions of the good life. Just as the barbarian invasions swept away the moral certainties of the Roman educated classes, so we have lost the certainties politicians clumsily invoke as 'Victorian values' – more the certainties of George Eliot's villain Bulstrode than of her heroines. Today's Dorothea, the argument goes, will only espouse what is true for her, and go out of her way to emphasize that she would not prescribe it for anyone else. Were she foolish enough to get entangled with a Casaubon, she would move out the moment the scales fell from her eyes. The one unforgiveable sin for her is not injustice or lack of integrity but intolerance. Out goes commitment and moral seriousness and in comes irony; out goes virtue and in comes polymorphous pleasure; out goes ethics and in comes aesthetics. 'Whatever turns you on' is our ethical bottom line. Not *Middlemarch* but John Updike's *Couples* (1968) or *Rabbit is Rich* (1982) speak of where our society finds itself. The traditions of life which shaped Caleb Garth have disappeared. We live instead with a lack of structure and form which would have astonished our ancestors and which leaves us 'defenceless to the casual flow of stimuli' (Gehlen, *Man in the Age of Technology*, 1980). In the West we have a narcissistic culture, radically individualized and rotten with sentimentality.

Because moral agency is always socially embodied we learn about the morality a society really subscribes to, as opposed to what it pays lip service to, through social analysis. It was on the grounds of his social analysis that Marx used to roar with laughter every time he heard the word 'morality'. He rejected what was propagated as morality as 'verbal trash' because it was so obviously inconsistent with the sheer cruelty of the factory system, and the ghastly living conditions of the working classes which the young Engels had described in words of fire in *The Conditions of the Working Class in England* (1845). Many of their contemporaries saw the point, and attempted their own descriptions of 'darkest England'. Conrad's *Heart of Darkness* (1902), as potent an omen of the coming darkness as Munch's, begins with the Thames flowing out to the sea, the great bearer of the traffic of empire, but with the dense smoke and darkness of London rising like a pall behind the storytellers. Real darkness, Conrad saw, was not in 'naked and uncivilized' Africa, but in the heart of the Western entrepreneur, driven mad by the quest for profit, setting himself up as a tribal deity to be worshipped. In 1914, twelve years after the book was published, Europe plunged into the darkness of Ypres and Passchendaele, the Marne and the Somme.

Conrad implies that if we ask what has led to the breakdown of moral consensus, to what MacIntyre calls the new Dark Ages, we have to look at the complex changes which began in the eighteenth century with the coming of industrial capitalism and which the Austrian economic historian Karl Polanyi called the Great Transformation. It is in this period that the fundamental means of production – land, labour and money itself – all become commodities, when rather than having markets – congenial places of exchange, as witnessed by the fine old 'market towns' of England, with their comfortable pubs and inns – we live in a 'market economy' and 'the market' has become a metaphor for the whole of life. This is not, of course, the cause of all the ills of the present century. On the other hand, its impact as the solvent of traditional moralities cannot be underestimated, as our growing understanding of the consequences of globalization makes clear.

One reason for Marx's notorious hostility to any moralizing was that he had no interest in portraying this historical movement, nor the entrepreneurs involved in it, as uniquely vicious. On the contrary, he was as convinced as right-wing apologists like Friedrich von Hayek or Francis Fukuyama that only capitalism could deliver the goods. His difference from them was in believing that it was only a transitional stage. In achieving the goal of human freedom, he believed, moral sermons had no place, and so the utopian and Christian Socialists were the targets of his fiercest satire. But perhaps his indifference to ethical theory was a real blind spot, for he failed to see that the process of achieving freedom itself might either permanently distort or even destroy the human project. For industrialization has led inexorably to urbanization which has resulted, two hundred years later, in more than half the world's populations living in great cities. This in turn has led to the loss of community, the growth of a sense of anomie and isolation, the rise in suicide that sparked the interest of the great French sociologist, Emil Durkheim (1858–1917). It has led to the disintegration of the peasant cultures of Europe, and increasingly of the rest of the world, embodying as they did the shared folk wisdom (and prejudices) of thousands of years. Peasant cultures, it has been argued by R. Critchfield (*The Villagers*, 1994), are humankind's finest achievement, for they were cultures which respected local habitat and ancestral ways, restrained individual self-seeking, and cultivated a sober and earthy ethic. The collapse of these cultures was accompanied by the rise of bureaucracy (to deal with the new mass structures) and of managerialism and the ethic of manipulation ('getting things done through people'). The history of Europe and of the Mediterranean basin had, of course, been a history of wars and competition for territory from time immemorial, but with the arrival of advanced capitalism, competition became the universal ethos, playing a crucial role in the genesis of both World Wars. War, class war, violence to the environment, manifold forms of creative destruction, have been the flowing robes of this particular historical movement. Small wonder, then, that it is plausible to talk of moral collapse.

Ethics and Social Justice

Written records of human community go back just over three millennia, and the languages in which they express themselves tell us of their vital needs. Equatorial languages, like Tamil for example, have no word for snow, for obvious reasons, while the language of the Inuit has many. But all languages quite soon find a need for the word 'justice' as a fundamental component of what it is that keeps human life flourishing. At the same time, arguments about what actually constitutes justice can be found in some of our most ancient texts. For both Europe and the Arab world one of the most influential discussions of the meaning of justice is that of Aristotle, in the fourth century before Christ. According to him, justice was the coping stone of the virtues, 'the actual exercise of complete excellence' precisely because it was about human relationships. In his *Nicomachean Ethics* he described it as 'exercising excellence' towards others, working for the common advantage of all – in other words, nurturing community. Later he has another stab at a definition in terms of a more ancient, and fundamental, hunch about the nature of justice as that which rewards the deserving and yet respects human equality. This latter point still forms the substance of much of our discussion of criminal justice. Unequal treatment of the same offence in different parts of the country leads us to say that justice has been outraged. Justice demands equal treatment for equal offences. And the 'equality before the law' that we take to be a *sine qua non* of justice actually marks an advance on Aristotle, for he insisted that justice meant equality only between equals, and thus not between free men and slaves, or between men and women.

For John Gray, (*The Moral Foundations of Market Institutions*, 1992), it is counter-intuitive to suggest that justice demands equality because an equal allocation between people would neglect considerations of what we deserve as well as of what we need – a view Aristotle would have commended. But of course what is intuitive is a matter of fundamental cultural presuppositions. Although he debated the issue it was counter-intuitive to Aristotle to believe that all human beings were equal: there were those by nature who were 'animated instruments' – slaves. The framers of the American constitution believed something similar about African slaves and Native Americans, whom George Washington called 'beasts of prey' and thought were destined to disappear. One of the major impacts of Christianity, (despite its flagrant denial in practice by the church), has been to insist that all human beings are equal as equal creatures of the one God, and equal sisters and brothers of the Son of Man. If the leaders did not heed it, the poor did. It was this theological idea that underlay the complaint of the poll tax protestors in 1381: 'When Adam delved and Eve span/Who was then the gentleman?' In the face of an elaborate and articulate ideology of hierarchy this stubborn belief in equality never disappeared, but was found amongst dissenting movements like the sixteenth-century Anabaptists, the seventeenth-century Diggers, and the Muggletonians to whom William Blake's mother belonged. The nineteenth-century Socialists generalized from equality before the law (which critics saw to be a fiction) to equality in other matters: hence the campaigns for votes for all, union rights and Henry George's plea for land reform.

Two rather different intuitions, or hunches, about the nature of justice are worth noting. The first is that of Aristotle's teacher, Plato, for whom justice was a matter of proper relations between both the different parts of the community and the different parts of the individual soul. What today we might call integrity or 'being a whole person' was essential, in his view, to the well-being of the community: a community of fragmented, disordered selves could not possibly be just.

The other insight derives from the Hebrew Bible, in which justice consists, in the first instance, in loyalty to the covenant which binds two parties. When one of the two parties is Yahweh, the God who frees slaves, then justice is seen to involve standing up for the poor. 'Give justice to the weak and the orphan,' says the Psalm 82. 'Maintain the right of the lowly and the destitute. Rescue the weak and the needy; deliver them from the hand of the wicked.' This is not the impartial and blindfolded justice in whose name the poor were hanged and transported in their thousands in eighteenth-century England, and which continues to imprison the poor throughout the world today, while turning a blind eye to corporate or political crime. On the contrary, it is justice which takes sides and thumps the oppressor. It was this partial or impassioned kind of justice that fired Engels in 1845 when he spoke of the indignation which arose from the contradiction of the human nature of the working class on the one hand and their condition of life, 'which is the outright, resolute and comprehensive negation of that nature' (*The Conditions of the Working Class in England*, 1845). This tradition of justice, an endangered species in a postmodern world, has recently found a passionate re-statement in John Pilger's *Hidden Agendas* (1998).

What Engels and Pilger give voice to, in the tradition of the Hebrew prophets, is often called social justice, something which is dismissed as a mischievous mirage by free-market apologists like Hayek and his numerous followers. This theoretical dismissal, and its practical denial by every capitalist economy constitutes, I shall argue, both the heart of the new Dark Ages 'already upon us', and in various ways the key ethical challenge of the period which faces us. For that very reason, it is instructive to see the extent to which Hayek agrees with both Aristotle and Marx and therefore to understand precisely where understandings of justice disagree. Material equality, Hayek tells us, would be a 'necessary postulate' if the shares of different individuals or groups were determined by deliberate human decision:

> In a society in which this were an unquestioned fact, justice would indeed demand that the allocation of the means for the satisfaction of human needs were effected according to some uniform principle such as merit or need . . . and that, where the principle adopted did not justify a difference, the shares of different individuals should be equal.
>
> (*The Mirage of Social Justice*, 1976)

In other words, social justice is fine in the face-to-face society. It is the changes accompanying Polanyi's Great Transformation which render social justice a nonsense. In what Hayek likes to call the Great or Open Society, older ethical rules no longer obtain, and for two reasons. One is a question of scale. In the world of competing international states and vast crowds there is a necessary reduction of the range of duties we owe to others. Hayek recognizes that the altruistic virtues are deeply ingrained, perhaps innate, but we have to allow rational insight to dominate inherited instincts, for altruism could get in the way of competition, and thus harm the Open Society. Like George Eliot, he recognizes that we are embarked on a 'great moral adventure', but for him it is not the incalculable diffusion of the virtues but the replacement of the intimate by the Open Society. This is threatened when we apply to all our fellow human beings rules that are appropriate only to the fellow members of a tribal group.

The second reason for the dismissal of social justice is that in a market society allocative decisions are not made by individuals; it is the impersonal operation of the market which allots goods and services to people, and this can be neither just nor unjust because the results were neither intended nor foreseen. The responsibility for the creation of a just society therefore, which for Aristotle was the key human political task, is rendered impossible by the way the market operates, though the market (and here Hayek agrees with Marx) does eventually deliver the optimum progress human beings can hope for.

Part of the Great Transformation has been a huge change in our understanding of what it means to be human. Humans are political animals, said Aristotle in his *Politics*, because they necessarily seek fellowship and then have to devise orderly ways of living together: 'When several villages are united in a single complete community, large enough to be nearly or quite self-sufficing, the state comes into existence, orginating in the bare needs of life, and continuing in existence for the sake of the good life.' What has replaced this vision in our own society is that of the autonomous individual. Autonomy, says John Gray, who until recently was an enthusiast for the priority of the market, is that situation in which a person can exercise choices in regard to capacities and resources in which they have a reasonable measure of success, unfettered by coercion. Only the market enables this. Only this allows the individual 'to act upon his own goals and values, his objectives and his plan of life, without subordination to any other individual or subjection to any collective decision procedure' (*Moral Foundations*, 1992). In 1992 Gray was prepared to speak of the values of 'autonomy, human solidarity and community' in one breath and to claim that autonomous men and women 'typically' emerge from strong communities and remain embedded in them. He followed Hayek in dismissing the idea that justice is the first virtue of political institutions regarding it rather as 'a far humbler affair, an artefact of the common life, a remedial virtue in which unfairness is corrected'. His current assessment of the way in which the operations of the global market have produced 'dislocation, social chaos and political instability' seems much nearer the mark (*False Dawn*, 1998). It is clear that any 'community' produced by market 'values' has little to do with Aristotle's search for the good life, or the communities which nourish the virtues, but is rather a way of describing the arena in which individuals follow their own idea of the good life and in which political institutions exist 'to provide that degree of order which makes such self-determined activity possible' (MacIntyre, *After Virtue*, 1985).

St Augustine famously described states without justice as 'nothing but robber bands'. If to live in a world without justice is to live in a world terrorized by Huns and Vandals – a Dark Age – and if we believe that to be intolerable then what should we do? As in that earlier period, Alastair MacIntyre suggested in 1981, people of good will need to turn to the construction of new forms of community within which civility and intellectual and moral life can be sustained in the new Dark Ages. And the prospect is bleak for, 'This time . . . the barbarians are not waiting beyond the frontiers; they have already been governing us for quite some time.' But perhaps a better alternative is to struggle for the reconstruction of justice and, as that implies, for an alternative view of the person and of community. While there is much in the present world disorder which flouts any notion of justice, this is not without powerful countervailing forces. Thus Paul Heelas, for example, argues that a crucial part of our world is the emergence of an international humanism, articulated above all in the United Nations Declaration of Human Rights, which forms 'a dominant tradition of our times' (*Detraditionalization*, 1996). 'The importance attached to equal opportunities or to positive discrimination . . . the role played by bodies such as the European Human Rights Commission, the establishment of the category "crimes against humanity", the development of prizes . . . for contributions to "humanity", and the activities of human rights groups, all serve to indicate the extent to which the ethic has become institutionalized.'

MacIntyre now shares the view of the great Utilitarian thinker, Jeremy Bentham, that the discourse of rights is 'nonsense on stilts', and understands it as an attempt to protect autonomy, little more than a protest against manipulation by others. In his view no good reasons for believing in human rights as such have ever been advanced. But

Heelas does not confine himself to this discourse, but points rather to a sense of human equality, by now very deeply entrenched across the majority of world cultures, which actually underpins the language of rights. And, if we look at the arguments of someone like the eighteenth-century evangelical John Newton, former slave-trader turned abolitionist, we can see that the emerging discourse of human rights was never just a defence of autonomy, but looked rather to a theologically grounded belief in human dignity which went back to the Israelites' exile in Egypt. In other words, it represents a legitimate development of one of those traditions which make possible the virtues which MacIntyre defends. When the framers of the American Constitution spoke of 'self-evidence' they appealed to what was self-evident to those whose grandparents and great grandparents included the Puritans of New England. It was only 'self-evident' within that frame of reference. Marx appealed to this same tradition of human dignity in speaking of a 'categorical imperative to overthrow all relations in which man is a debased, enslaved, forsaken and despicable creature' ('Contribution to a Critique of Hegel's Philosophy of Law', 1844). The imperative assumes, of course, that human beings are not supposed to be debased, enslaved and despised, an assumption about the equal dignity of all human beings derived from this much older tradition, and a tradition which had no interest whatever in autonomy as such. According to Hayek there are no possible norms of social justice which apply across the international sphere, and to claim that there are is humbug, but the work of Amnesty International, of UNICEF and of the United Nations Commission on Human Rights seems to disprove this. What has in fact happened is that an originally theologically grounded understanding of human dignity has been universally exported. The universalization of this assumption has huge implications for our understanding of social justice, and therefore for our assessment of the workings of the world economy. It is these implications that I want to go on to explore.

Chapter 2

THE MIDAS TOUCH

Capitalism is at one and the same time the best thing that has ever happened to the human race, and the worst.

Frederic Jameson, *Postmodernism*, 1991

Greed and the Good Life

The purpose of political society, says Aristotle, is to go beyond the bare necessities of life to the good life. The good life by no means excludes the goods of culture, sport or the table – on the contrary. On the other hand it was, for Aristotle, inconceivable without the practice of the virtues. So the good life meant a moral life, a life in which courage, temperance and magnanimity could flourish. Any of the vices could destroy the good life, but above all *pleonexia* (acquisitiveness, the greed that knows no limit), along with lawlessness, is the very opposite of justice.

The vision of the good life has known many transformations. The monastic ideal, for instance, which began before the barbarian invasions of the fourth century AD, and reached its peak between the eleventh and thirteenth centuries, was so chary of the pleasures of the flesh that Satan might come tempting the monk with a dish of lentils – not something we automatically associate with high living. The chivalric version privileged a certain kind of courage in a way which has more in common with the heroic society of the Norse epics than with Aristotle. The version which marks our own society is, as we would expect, connected with the Great Transformation. Unlike any earlier society we do not 'have' but we 'are' an economy. In this situation the good life comes to be decisively tied up with consumption and growth and, as Aristotle predicted, acquisitiveness preys like a cancer on justice.

At the end of the twentieth century, Michael Redclift remarks (*Wasted*, 1996) that consumption is worshipped, almost as an alternative to democracy. Not just as an alternative to democracy, we should add, but as an account of the very meaning of life. Many people have observed how over the past forty years we have ceased to be citizens, whose primary duty is to build and share in the community, and have become consumers instead, whose primary duty it is to buy. The very nature of our economy demands, says Victor Lebow, a leading retail analyst, (in Pilger, *Hidden Agendas*), 'that we make consumption our way of life, that we convert the buying and use of goods into rituals, that we seek spiritual satisfaction, our ego satisfaction, in consumption'. In *How Much is Enough?* (1992) Alan Thein Durning cites the Range Rover advertisement that appeared in the United States in the midst of the 1990 recession: 'Buy Something. Our preference, of course, would be that you buy a Range Rover. But if that's not in the cards, buy a microwave. A basset hound. Theatre tickets. A Tootsie roll. Something.' The message is that there is a straight choice between consumption and disaster. The way in which we shop, especially at the big holidays, shows the extent to which we have internalized that.

The dangers of the idolatry of consumption were hardly part of fourth-century BC Greek life, but Aristotle saw very clearly where *pleonexia* could lead. In his remarks on running the household (*oikonomia*) he makes a sharp distinction between money-making on the one hand and economics, which is making the necessary provision for the 'household', on the other. Daly and Cobb in *For the Common Good* (1990) summarize the distinction thus: first, it takes the long rather than the short view; second, it considers costs and benefits to the whole community, not just to the parties to the transaction; and third, it focuses on concrete use value and the limited accumulation thereof, rather than on abstract value and its impetus toward unlimited accumulation.

The distinction was crucially important for Aristotle because it involved the very heart of his understanding of what it meant to be human. For him the good life, and being a whole human being, *essentially involved the acceptance of limits.* St Paul's 'Let your moderation be known to all' was good Aristotelian advice. The sordid business of lending on interest was not part of genuine economics as far as Aristotle was concerned because it lost sight of limits. It represented an unnatural fetishization of money, divorced from the question of use value, the contribution to the good of the community. He recognized that because the desires of the human heart were infinite there were those for whom the chief business of life might be accruing wealth, making money out of money. His comment on such people was to include the Midas story in his account of economics. Midas, the original fat cat, wanted everything he touched to turn to gold. His wish was granted, and he starved to death. The story is a parable of what happens when consumption and acquisitiveness become the centre of life, as they do in a capitalist economy.

Being human involves accepting limits, as is well known to any artist, or musician, or any academic for that matter. Nothing worthwhile is achieved without recognizing them and indeed we only exist within very specific limits. Money, however, because it is a mathematical quantity and not a sum of cows or corn, or silk or sand, seems to escape these limits. 'The peculiarity of money', noted Lewis Mumford in *The Pentagon of Power* (1970), 'is that it knows no biological limits or ecological restrictions. When the Augsburg financier, Jakob Fugger the Elder, was asked when he would have so much money that he would feel no need for more, he replied, as all great magnates tacitly or openly do, that he never expected such a day to come.' It is this quest for more which constitutes the spiritual centre of our world. It is an economy which is an anti-economy, a limitless craving which is the shadow of genuine satisfaction. A meeting of economists in 1987 rejected the very idea of limits which could not be taken care of by capital (Daly and Cobb, *For the Common Good*). Why? Belief in the possibility of unlimited growth is the very foundation of the ideological doctrine of corporate libertarianism, says David Korten, the former development worker turned radical critic, because to accept the reality of physical limits is to accept the need to limit greed and acquisition in favour of economic justice and sufficiency (*When Corporations Rule the World,* 1995). However, it is important to realize that it is not just about society, or the global economy, being driven by a group of exceptionally greedy individuals. On the contrary, the need to grow is part of the internal logic of capitalism, as necessary to it as petrol is to the combustion engine. Since in a global economy we are all caught up in this willy-nilly, it is essential to try and understand the nature of the compulsion.

The Growth Compulsion

Although we have lived with capitalism now for two hundred years, there is no agreement on what constitutes the compulsion to expand. Instead we have to collate the suggestions both advocates and critics have made. The first of these, to which Adam Smith draws attention in *The Wealth of Nations* (1776), is the impact of the *division of labour*. In subsistence economies people might reckon to provide most of the necessaries of life themselves, but as he illustrates, this is often a very inefficient process. To take his famous example: working on their own a person might make only two score pins a day, but when the operations are broken down in a small pin-making factory each person is responsible for nearly five thousand pins per day. Specialization, then, is efficient (though there are questions about unemployment and the worth of the product), but if the workers at the pin-making factory are to increase their income they can only do so by making and selling more pins. In a society where everyone is a specialist, everyone is caught in the same spiral. Only by making more, selling more and consuming more can we improve our 'standard of living': the consumer society is born. As Daly puts it, 'After specialization a country is no longer free *not* to trade.' (*Beyond Growth,* 1996.) The economist celebrates the miracle of 'circular flow': through consumption households support businesses which provide work for households. Commodities and money form a perfect model of perpetual motion, a model which expands through investment. Only a common agreement that 'enough was enough' and the attainment of perfect equilibrium between all specializations would stop the treadmill. Or, of course, the recognition of the significance of entropy, to which we will return.

Polanyi, in *The Great Transformation* (1944), ties the need for growth more tightly to the advent of *machinery*. Machines are expensive and their purchase and use can only be justified if sales and the provision of raw materials are reasonably guaranteed. Again there is a spiral. Machines have to produce more to pay for themselves. Mass production can only succeed where there is mass consumption. Those with money have to be persuaded to buy, or new markets have to be found if the immediate one is satiated. So begins the restless search for ever-new markets.

According to Joseph Schumpeter, another Viennese economist who came to the United States shortly before the Second World War, it is *innovation* which is the basic motor of growth. Growth is not just driven by the need for new markets, but by competition provided by new commodities, new technologies, new sources of supply, new modes of organization. Profit is needed for the research and development to keep ahead. Competition demands new, more efficient machines, more capital, and wider markets. 'Under the lash of competition', commented Ernest Mandel, who in this respect agreed with Schumpeter, 'the capitalist mode of production . . . becomes the first mode of production in the history of mankind the essential aim of which appears to be *unlimited increase in production*, constant accumulation of capital by the capitalization of the surplus value produced in the course of production itself.' (*Marxist Economic Theory*, 1968.) For Schumpeter, capitalism is the process of creative destruction which is triggered by new methods of production to begin an endlessly restless process. At the heart of the process is the entrepreneur, who seizes on a new idea, exploits it, and drives the old from the field. Characteristically there is a life-cycle to the whole process, marked by rapid growth to begin with, a slow-down and decline before the advent of new products or technologies.

Finally, growth is also demanded by the *system of interest*. If we borrow money to finance plant and machinery, we have to make a profit to pay back the loan and the interest. Failure to make a profit threatens the entire system. It means that less money for investment is available, which may mean job losses, which in turn means that consumers have less money to spend, leading to further cut-backs and job losses and so on. The downward spiral is reflected in falling tax receipts for the government, reduced social spending and, the ultimate nightmare of all economists, the moment when recession turns into fully fledged depression.

As economists have known from Marx onwards, this drive for growth is not only exceptionally dynamic, it is at the same time profoundly unstable. Talk of 'global meltdown' has accompanied the Asian crisis. Now it is surmised that if Iran and Iraq re-join the oil-exporting markets then prices could fall drastically, and falling commodity prices, Alex Brummer reminds us, were a precursor of the Wall Street crash (*Guardian*, 3 June 1998). 'The markets' constantly have the jitters and the possibility of the global financial system collapsing is evidently real.

Reasons for Believing

The reasons for commitment to growth and consumption are clear enough: just look around! Look at the staggering changes capitalism has been responsible for since the end of the eighteenth century. These changes are usually described as an enormous rise in 'the standard of living'. Some critics argue that medieval society made a better job of caring for the poor than modern society, and Lewis Mumford made a persuasive case for considering the medieval city the most attractive urban environment yet known. There is no doubt that the early stages of industrialization, wherever and whenever they occur, do inflict appalling hardships on the poor, and that by comparison life in the village may be better. That the poverty of subsistence may be preferable to the misery of today's shanty towns or yesterday's Western industrial slums has been argued recently by Vandana Shiva. Western observers, such as the officials of the International Monetary Fund (IMF), she argues, believe any non-participation in the world economy to be poverty, whereas it may in fact be 'prudent subsistence'. The Ethiopian famine, in which 100,000 people died, was partly created by the attempt to remove culturally perceived poverty. 'The displacement of nomadic Afars from their traditional pastureland . . . by commercial agriculture (financed by foreign companies) led to their struggle for survival in the fragile uplands which degraded the ecosystem and led to the starvation of cattle and the nomads.' (*Staying Alive*, 1989.)

These observations are important, but they do not, of course, amount to a romanticization of the pre-industrial past. One of the best known comparisons of pre- and post-industrial societies, Peter Laslett's *The World We Have Lost* (1965), records many instances of savagely inhumane conditions of life in seventeenth-century Britain, for instance. There is little doubt that in terms of the 'basic indicators', child and maternal mortality, average life expectancy and basic education, post-industrial human beings are far better off than their predecessors. Improvements in diet mean that people live longer on average, and are taller and sturdier. Statistics from the Food and Agriculture Organization in 1997 tell us that calories consumed per head are 27 per cent higher in the South than they were in 1963, and that deaths from famine, starvation and malnutrition are fewer than ever before. On the other side is the sad statistic that one third of United States citizens suffer from obesity.

Housing for the majority is certainly better. While the constraints of industrial discipline were absent in pre-industrial society there was also much remorseless toil, especially for those, usually just referred to in contemporary documents as 'poor folk', who could not take servants for granted. Doubtless some labour-saving devices are instruments of our 'elegant estrangement', as E.J. Mishan calls it in *The Costs of Economic Growth* (1967), but there are many others which have made a real contribution to the quality of life. Since 1960 child-mortality rates around the world have halved and malnutrition has been cut by a third. Above all, the advance of medical research and skill has saved people from the everyday killers of only half a century ago – diphtheria, smallpox, typhoid and tuberculosis. It is true that, although many major diseases have been more or less eradicated, there is now serious concern about new strains of TB and malaria resistant to conventional treatments, and there has been a rise, in Britain at least, in cases of asthma and other allergies, in cancer, in new diseases like AIDS, and in so-called diseases of affluence, like coronary thrombosis. A pessimist might claim that gains and losses here amount to a zero-sum equation, but any inspection of nine-teenth-century hospital records, with their appalling child- and maternal-mortality rates, makes this implausible. And those of us who take high-quality dentistry for granted need only go back to Dorothy Wordsworth's diary, written in 1802, to recall the misery of life without it: looking in the mirror at the age of forty she saw a trim and fit figure but the toothless face of an old woman. When teeth were pulled out to deal with toothache, people not infrequently bled to death. We should not hesitate to call progress in dental science real progress.

By any standards, one of the most important innovations of the twentieth century has been the creation of cheap and effective contra-ception which has saved women from the burden of unending childbirth. Feminism, the most important social revolution of the twentieth century, which marks the beginning of the dismantling of patriarchy, would have had a very different history without this, and some of the technological changes already mentioned. In addition, the rise of universal education, of democratic systems where both women and men have the vote, of effective communication across continents, a great increase in leisure time, all this would not have been possible without the industrial revolution, cruelly as it treated those at the bottom of the pile. And those things which give us some of the great-est pleasure in life, such as music-making or art, or theatre, all require some degree of surplus. These existed before the Industrial Revolu-tion, of course, but it is the surplus that democratized them. As Schumpeter insists, 'Not only modern technology and economic orga-nization, but all the features and achievements of modern civilization are, directly or indirectly, the products of the capitalist process. They must be included in any balance sheet of it and any verdict about its deeds or misdeeds.'

Schumpeter also claims that there was never so much personal freedom of mind and body as in capitalist society – ironically, an opinion voiced just before the advent of McCarthyism. But it is capital-ism, in this view, which frees us from fate (for example, bad harvests, or the limitations of harnessable energy) and allows us to take charge of our own destiny. This is why US President Harry Truman could insist that, 'All freedom is dependent on freedom of enterprise.' For right-wing economists like Hayek (another Austrian), Friedman, and their followers, the 'free' market, without controls or interventions, is the only guarantee of political freedom. The moral and the market economy are one and the same thing, because they enable 'choice'. By virtue of the magic of the market, say Milton and Rose Friedman, 'no external force, no coercion, no violation of freedom is necessary to produce co-operation among individuals all of whom can benefit' (*Free to Choose*, 1990). Freedom, then, rather narrowly defined as the freedom of those with cash to spend, is our ethical bottom line, our absolute.

Reasons for Doubt

Market enthusiasts insist that the gains of the past two centuries are a package deal, tied to the capitalist system. All but the wilder apologists for capitalism acknowledge that there may be bad side-effects as well, but judge them worth the cost. In Hayek's terms, we have to think of human history in terms of a moving column. Those at the front may suffer, but those coming later reap the benefits (again we note a similarity with Marx's view). One of the problems is that those who make this judgment are not usually those at the receiving end, and there is ample evidence for the other half of Jameson's remark, used as an epigraph for this chapter, that capitalism is not just the best but also the worst thing ever to happen to us. There are no advances, except perhaps in medicine, that come without their disadvantages. Most are attended by deep shadows to left and to right. We have, of course, to remember the state of those currently at the front of Hayek's column in the South (the so-called 'developing countries'), and amongst the third generation unemployed in the North (the affluent world), but even for those reaping the benefits of consumerism, there are deep ambiguities. We have to consider the impact of growth on our communities and our understanding of what it means to be human, on our cultures, and, the bottom line, on the environment.

Take, for example, the central contention that the market enhances our freedom. Writing in 1944 in the context of the struggle against Fascism (and as Western economists met at Bretton Woods to inaugurate what became the World Bank and the IMF), Polanyi came to the opposite conclusion. For Friedman it is of the first importance that politics and economics are separated. Such a separation characterized Victorian society and posed, says Polanyi in his book *The Great Transformation*, 'a deadly danger to the substance of society', which almost automatically produced personal moral freedom at the expense of justice and security. Liberal freedom degenerates into a mere advocacy of free enterprise, reduced to a fiction by giant trusts and monopolies. For him such freedom is almost certain to end in Fascism, a claim to which I shall return in Chapter 5.

We might argue about that, but the effect of the consumer society on morality has long been evident. At the very beginning of our era, when the Great Transformation was only just beginning, the Dutch physician Bernard Mandeville noted in his famous poem *The Fable of the Bees* that it is vanity, greed and fornication which keep us all busy. Imagine a city where there were none of these things: a sleepy place with mass unemployment and indeed starvation.

> As Pride and Luxury decrease,
> So by degrees they leave the Seas.
> Not Merchants now; but Companies
> Remove whole Manufactures.
> All Arts and Crafts neglected lie;
> Content the Bane of Industry,
> Makes 'em admire their homely Store,
> And neither seek, nor covet more.
> So few in the vast Hive remain;
> The Hundredth part they can't maintain
> Against th'Insults of numerous Foes;
> Whom yet they valiantly oppose:
> Till some well-fenced Retreat is found;
> And here they die, or stand their Ground.

The moral is clear: moralists can huff and puff, but, on a cool reckoning, private vices are public benefits in the sense that without them there is no growth. We can apply his reasoning to the present debate about pornography. In 1990 sales of 'top-shelf magazines' in Britain were estimated at 2.25 million copies per month, making a total gross profit of £23 million per year. Paul Raymond, the publisher of many of these, is amongst the UK's richest men. Plenty of growth, of course, and splendid for GNP (Gross National Product), but vehemently opposed by the feminism which growth has also made possible, as well as by many other groups in society.

In the eighteenth century, Mandeville was duly condemned from a thousand pulpits, and in Ireland had his book burnt by the common hangman, but his lesson was learnt, among others, by someone who began by opposing him – Adam Smith. Aristotle believed that speech was given us to form community, but for Smith speech was part of our 'propensity to barter, truck and exchange one thing for another'. So for Smith it was not the polity which came first, but the market. We see how the community that nourishes the virtues is displaced by this loose agglomerate of individuals in trade. Doubtless led on by the flow of his argument, Smith abandoned the elaborate cautions of his moral philosophy and famously observed that it is not to the benevolence of the butcher that we owe our dinner, but to the appeal to his self-interest. Shorn of Smith's assumptions about the priority of moral sympathy, *Homo sapiens* is reduced to *Homo economicus*, the rational utility maximizer, of whom it is assumed that self-interest, expressed primarily through the quest for financial gain, is his main concern. This evolutionary freak has next to no use for community as Margaret Thatcher's infamous remark, 'There is no such thing as society,' spelt out. Competition is his metier, not co-operation, and he measures progress by increased consumer spending.

Sociological and psychological studies, however, seem to confirm Aristotle's view that we are indeed community animals. We are not 'individuals' but persons in relation to each other. The only absolutely 'individual' thing about us is a corpse. When the old close-knit community is replaced by the anonymous world of the city or large town dominated by the car, the superstore and 'personal entertainment', the very structures of society start to break down and, as sociologists since Durkheim have recognized, there are rises in suicide, crime and 'motiveless' violence. A century after Durkheim, in 1982, Edward Schwarz, an American sociologist, comments, 'It now appears certain that a strong, local community is essential to psychological well-being, personal growth, social order, and a sense of political effi-ciency.' (Daly and Cobb, *For the Common Good*.) And Robert Bellah and his colleagues note that, 'Americans have pushed the logic of exploitation about as far as it can go. It seems to lead not only to failure at the highest levels . . . but also to personal and familial breakdown.' (*The Good Society*, 1991.) Already in the 1840s Karl Marx had taken over the word 'alienation' to describe what happens in the world where *Homo economicus* is king. To be sure, it has to be recognized that many of the old small communities could also be deeply oppressive for those who did not fit in and that they functioned to keep everyone in their place. Their passing has meant not just anonymity but the dismantling of the old system of hierarchy and deference, which could be gain or loss depending on your point of view (I, for one, applaud). However, a century after the replacement of the local by the anonymous society was first the subject of systematic reflection, we have not just the disintegration of community but its replacement by the market. As the campaigning journalist Jeremy Seabrook put it, writing of Britain, children are now stripped of all social influence save that of the market-place:

> The individual is denuded of everything but appetites, desires, tastes, wrenched from any context of human obligation or commitment. It is a process of mutilation; and once this has been achieved, we are offered the consolation of reconstituting the abbreviated humanity out of the things and the goods around us, and the fantasies and vapours they emit.
>
> (*What Went Wrong?*, 1978)

In Britain the level of participation has fallen in almost all voluntary groups. 'Even the local pub has suffered, with more people preferring to drink at home. There has been a major cultural shift away from seeking recreation with one's neighbours and towards finding it with one's friends or, more often, at home with the television.' (Douthwaite, *The Growth Illusion*, 1992.) Crime has been shown to rise with economic growth, leading to further social disintegration as people feel more insecure in their neighbourhoods. Property crime accounts for about 90 per cent of the total by the late 1980s, clearly suggesting, as Douthwaite observes, that most crime has an economic motive and is not aberrant or irrational behaviour.

Perhaps the disintegration of intimate communities was inevitable, and, as we have seen, there were gains as well as losses. It is another matter, however, that the market has become the matrix of our interactions. When this happens the interests of money take priority over people, a fact shown only too clearly by what has happened vis-à-vis world debt in the past twenty years. In such a situation we lose our way. In 1961 Lewis Mumford anticipated MacIntyre's bleak vision in his great book, *The City in History*. He compared Western civilization to a gigantic motor car moving along a one-way road at an ever-accelerating speed.

> Unfortunately as now constructed the car lacks both steering-wheel and brakes, and the only form of control the driver exercises consists in making the car go faster, though in his fascination with the machine itself and his commitment to achieving the highest speed possible, he has quite forgotten the purpose of the journey. This state of helpless submission to the economic and technological mechanisms modern man has created is curiously disguised as progress, freedom, and the mastery of man over nature. As a result, every permission has become a morbid compulsion. Modern man has mastered every creature above the level of the viruses and bacteria – except himself.

The primary casualty of the whole process has always been the poor, as the radical journalist John Pilger graphically describes in his writings today, but, on a more abstract level, our understanding of the human project or 'the purpose of the journey' has also been a casualty.

One of the most vivid illustrations of the way in which the consumer society reconstructs the human image was offered by Vance Packard in his 1957 classic *The Hidden Persuaders*. He showed how the advertising industry effectively makes a mockery of the claim that the consumer society expands our freedom of choice. Led by 'motivational research' analysts, Packard showed how advertisers were able to turn around failing products simply by changing the shape of labels. We instinctively believe this to be impossible, but the statistics, and the vast revenues of the advertising industry, are there to show that it works. In 1989 global corporate spending on advertising, packaging and design amounted to $120 for every person in the world. In the United States expenditure rose from $198 per capita in 1950 to $495 in 1990. Packard's original study was done forty years ago, when advertising was still relatively unsophisticated, and when not yet 97 per cent of all households in the West owned a television. Its impact on our 'freedom to choose' may be assumed to be proportional.

Of course advertisers can ask what is wrong with persuasion: it goes on in a small way even in local markets. Ten years after Packard, the German sociologist W.F. Haug gave the answer in his *Critique of Commodity Aesthetics* (1967). Effectively, advertising turns us all into commodities. 'How is it that clever and competent people don't make it in their careers?' asked a wool advert. 'Don't call it bad luck it is only a matter of "packaging". You can sell yourself better in a new suit! And that is often what counts in life.' Christopher Lasch pointed out that what all this advertising hype generated was a 'culture of narcissism'. The narcissistic individual is uneasy about health, ageing and death, eager to get along with others but unable to make real friendships, and attempts to sell him- or herself as if he was a commodity. Appearance, display and the management of impressions are what count.

We mentioned that many medical advances were wholly beneficial. An exception is the vast increase in 'procedures' for cosmetic surgery, one of the fastest-growing areas in the USA. In 1990, 640,000 of these 'procedures' were carried out, the most frequent being liposuction (designed to reduce the layers of subcutaneous fat), breast augmentation and collagen injections: all these aim to make people, and especially women, more desirable commodities in the sexual market-place, conforming to the advertising image. The corollary to this is the rise in anorexia and bulimia, above all in young women, but now also seen in young men. 'The most massive exploitation of the body', writes John O'Neil, 'occurs whenever the economy teaches us to disvalue it in its natural state and to revalue it once it has been sold grace, spontaneity, vivaciousness, bounce, confidence, smooth-ness and freshness.' (*Five Bodies*, 1985.) The ordinary condition of men and women becomes a matter of shame, and as life becomes more sedentary the economy sells it back to us in fitness centres, aerobics and sport. Advertising does not just sell us products, but power, sexuality and freedom – the human image. The immense expense, effort and talent put into advertising suggests, as Daly and Cobb point out, that we are not really driven by self-interest and an insatiable desire for commodities after all, and that the growth economy only succeeds by a massive effort to reconstruct what it means to be human.

Looking at developments in the growth-driven world, the French social analyst and philosopher Jean Baudrillard argues that the world of use values has collapsed into the world of sign values. Images and signs dominate our lives to such an extent that the distinction between illusion and reality collapses – it is what he calls the world of 'hyper-reality', and, as we shall see, in the world of speculative finance this is exactly what has happened. He calls his book on the subject *Symbolic Exchange and Death* (1976), making the point that this disintegration of everything into a sign spells both the death of cultures and the death of the person. The economy no longer exists to serve human needs, but human needs have to be distorted to serve the expanding market. Saatchi and Saatchi's targeting of the children's market is a perfect illustration. Their mission is, they say, 'to connect our clients to the kid market, to match our clients' business objectives with the needs, drives and desires of kids.' (Pilger, *Hidden Agendas*, 1998.)

If this is what the growth economy does to community and the individual, it also spells death to much of our cultural heritage. Consider, for example, the impact of television, now so universal that

the Television Licensing Authority in Britain is incapable of believing
that you do not possess a set. Technically it is an amazing achievement, and as everyone says, the wildlife programmes are wonderful,
but otherwise does it really enrich our family and corporate life, and
nurture the human soul? Neil Postman, the Professor of Media
Studies at New York University, thinks not. He points out that a
whole series of studies found that in the United States, where the
average person watches seven hours of television a day, many of
the viewers could not recall a single item of news a few minutes after
watching it. The medium militates against careful exposition and
reasoned discourse and trivializes political discussion. 'When a population becomes distracted by trivia, when cultural life is redefined as a
perpetual round of entertainments, when serious public conversation
becomes a form of baby-talk, when, in short, a people become an
audience and their public business a vaudeville act, then a nation
finds itself at risk; culture-death is a clear possibility.' (*Amusing
Ourselves to Death*, 1987.)

Culture-death of another kind is also bound up with economic
growth. Bill Bryson, in his farewell tour of Britain in 1995 (*Notes from a
Small Island*), noted how all English towns now look the same – everywhere identical chain stores, shopping malls and precincts. Local
cultures which grew over more than a thousand years, building and
designing to accommodate local materials and local products, have all
become homogeneous. Mass production leads to a loss of individual-
ity, of craftsmanship, of local tastes and cuisines. Traditional music,
which was part of the same organic process, has likewise been swept
away by a deluge of synthesized sound. Standardization and unifor-
mity are the inevitable outcomes of a global economy dominated by
multinational corporations like Coca Cola or McDonald's. As the chief
executive of Heinz, Tony O'Reilly, put it: 'Once television is there,
people of whatever shade, culture, or origin want roughly the same
things.' This deadly and tedious homogenization of culture is now a
worldwide phenomenon, due especially to one of the largest of all
industries, tourism. When in 1967 E.J. Mishan complained that many
Mediterranean resorts had been spoilt, his critics accused him of

elitism. But tourism has now become a truly serious cultural problem, generating mass prostitution in Thailand, the Philippines, and now Costa Rica, the favourite child sex destination for the US, as well as devastating cultural erosion in places like Goa, where resistance groups have now been formed – with what chance, however, against the global might of the Western consumer? Whose choice is being expanded? Not that of the locals, whose prices are forced to rock bottom by that wonderful engine, competition, and whose water and other resources are used for the tourists. Even for the Westerner, what does such choice amount to if it is the freedom to travel from one identical city to another, to be able to visit McDonald's in Moscow, Delhi or London? What kind of choice is that?

And does all this consumer growth lead to a real increase in human happiness? Study after study has shown that it does not. It would be no surprise to any exponent of traditional wisdom to learn that the possession of more and more commodities does not make people happier. People remain aware that love, respect, doing something worthwhile are what really count, and yet they are somehow trapped in the consumerist web. Even our deepest relationships are the targets of consumer campaigns through Valentine's Day, Mother's Day, Father's Day, etc., so that if we do not spend money we feel that somehow we are failing. Looking at the results of studies in the United States on the relation between affluence and happiness in 1976, Scitovsky called the mass-produced culture of his day 'the joyless economy'. He compared the unimaginative culture and food of his country with that of Europe. Could he have anticipated that Europe, and the rest of the world, would rush to adopt it? Back in 1962 another advocate of the consumer economy, Sir Arthur Lewis, cheerfully recognized that growth did not necessarily bring happiness, but that it did after all enlarge our choice. 'Choice' is a key word amongst the moral marketeers. But aside from the fact that only those with money can choose, is choosing between 572 different models of car, as it was in 1992, an enrichment of life? Between forty television channels with a diet of identical news, B-movies and sport? And, given the joint forces of corporate monopoly and advertising, what does consumer sovereignty amount to?

The consumer economy has also made an unwelcome change in our attitude to our planet. As Wendell Berry puts it, under the prevailing economic values the stuff of creation is too cheap to care for. Pre-capitalist cultures had acquired over millennia a sense of discipline or modesty concerning needs articulated, for example, in the Puritan 'waste not, want not' ethic. Alison Uttley's *The Country Child*, an account of country childhood in Derbyshire at the end of the nineteenth century, records the frugal joys of middle-class life, with few luxuries and a rigorous prohibition of waste. To cut the knot on the string of a parcel, rather than to unpick it, was unheard of. This ethic obtained virtually worldwide, and remains where peasant cultures are still to be found. As Durning argues in *How Much is Enough?* (1992), consumerism, not moderation, is the aberrant value system. The consumer lifestyle is a radical departure from the conserving principles that human cultures developed over centuries. Conservation and moderation, however, spell suffocation to expanding markets. For these to survive, we have needed to develop, in little over half a century, built-in obsolescence, a throw-away culture, and a vast advertising industry whose task it is to convince us of needs we never knew we had. We are no longer able to distinguish what Keynes called absolute needs – for food, shelter, affection and so on – from the wants which define us in the consumerist pecking order. Wilfred Beckerman, an economist who mocks the environmental lobby, replied to this objection that *all* needs are socially constructed (*Small is Stupid*, 1995). Such a response is sufficient indication of the moral collapse such a culture brings.

Fair Shares and the Consumer Society

In *Moral Foundations* (1992) John Gray considered the pursuit of equality in the name of 'justice' a diversion from the proper task of improving human welfare. Those needs, which he calls basic needs, whose satisfaction is essential to the possibility of a worthwhile life, should indeed be satisfied, if necessary by welfare provision. Given this we have to recognize that, 'Unlike any political procedure for the allocation of resources, free markets enable individuals to command goods and services on their terms, and to exit from forms of provision that displease them.' In *False Dawn* (1998) he has changed his position and recognizes that, 'Free markets, the desolation of families and communities and the use of the sanctions of the criminal law against social collapse go in tandem.' The great majority of the human race are in no position to 'exit' from forms of provision which displease them. Sheer survival is the agenda.

In 1992 Gray advocated the benefits of the good life, rather than justice, but it is precisely because the market destroys justice that it cannot bring the good life to most people. In the last quarter of the twentieth century inequalities have increased between the rich nations and the poor, but also within the rich nations. Since 1979 in Britain, for example, 15 per cent of £31 billion in tax cuts have been diverted to the lower 50 per cent of income earners; 27 per cent went to the top one per cent. The report *Child Poverty and Deprivation in the UK* (1990) found that between 1979 and 1990 the number of children living in poverty had risen from 17 per cent to 28 per cent. In the same period in the United States the wealth of the top one per cent grew by 63 per cent, while that of the bottom 60 per cent declined. In Social Democratic Sweden by 1992 the richest 2 per cent of Swedish households accounted for 23 per cent of all the wealth in the country. One of the growth ideologists' greatest successes must be in making the idea of redistributive taxation unacceptable, and to create a climate where the use of tax havens and vast differentials between rich and poor is taken for granted. Many new jobs have been created in this period, but they have often been part-time, temporary and low-paid. Unsurprisingly it has been shown that there is a high correlation between job insecurity, psychological stress and high mortality rates.

If we turn to the global community, the Worldwatch Institute breaks down the world's population into three groups (in Durning, *How Much is Enough?*). The world's poor earn less than $700 a year per family member, walk everywhere and have an inadequate diet. The middle-income group earn between $700 and $7500 per family member, use public transport and have some amenities such as refrigerators or washing-machines. The consumer class travel in cars and planes and have all the consumer durables. It is this group primarily who are responsible for the doubling of per capita consumption of copper, energy, meat, steel and timber since mid-century, the quadrupling of car ownership and cement consumption and the huge increase in air travel. Such extraordinary growth is part of the logic of a system whose 'ultimate purpose' it is to produce more consumer goods. But what happens to us in a world where on the one hand luxuries are turned into necessities, and on the other 35,000 infants die every day from environmentally related diseases? What happens to our humanity when an American president, George Bush, can inform the world, in the face of compelling evidence of the global warming to which his country is the biggest single contributor, that, 'The American way of life [cheap petrol, cars, homes with all the labour-saving devices] is not negotiable.' What does this say about human solidarity and our understanding of the human project? Are we prepared to face what is implied if 'the American way of life' is not globally possible?

In 1992 Gray urged the concept of satiable needs against a 'corrosive spirit of comparison which has obscured our perception of what is truly good and bad in human lives' (*Moral Foundations*). Before he abandoned his faith in the 'free' market, his view was that we should not focus on justice, but on the 'real' content of the good life. It is important not to get lost in academic abstractions. John Pilger describes an eleven-year-old Punjabi girl who has gone blind, and who makes her living by stitching footballs: 'When asked about the fun of being a child, Sonia said there was no fun in what she did. "I have no choice," she said. It takes her a day to stitch two balls, for which she earns the equivalent of fifteen pence . . . not enough to buy a litre of milk.' In Gray's extraordinary terms, Sonia cannot 'exit' her situation and her 'autonomy' is limited. This kind of labour is part of the process of globalization in which clothing, sports goods and electronics are made in conditions of impoverishment and exploitation. It is, says Pilger, 'the confluence of globalization and state terror that defines the new Cold War'. Those who prize autonomy as the heart of morality, and who believe that the market makes it possible, do not see that the free market produces lives like Sonia's for most of the world's people, and that this autonomy is parasitic on the unfreedom of the poor. It is this that demands talk of justice, and that makes its rejection such an impertinence.

And there is a crucial problem with determining satiable needs. The whole human community, but especially those who drive the global economy, face a central conundrum, which is this: the world cannot provide the standard of living currently enjoyed by those in the consumer class for all earth's people. E.J. Mishan argues that even if an economic miracle were somehow to occur within a decade or two, as a result of which living standards in Third World countries approached those currently enjoyed in the affluent West, the huge increase in global consumption would devour such quantities of raw materials and create such vast amounts of industrial and domestic waste as to wreck the ecosystem within a few years. Are we then to reduce the population from the current level of 5.7 billion to the 2 billion which Cornell researchers calculate can be provided for if a less meat-intensive Mediterranean diet is adopted? What political decisions would enable that to happen? They predict severe social, economic and political conflicts plus catastrophic public health and environmental health problems if the population soars, as predicted, to 12 billion (Korten, *When Corporations Rule the World*, 1995). Can we rely on technical fixes to solve our problems as Julian Simon thinks, with his faith in 'the ultimate resource'? Herman Daly argues that simply stopping growth in rates of global pollution, ecological degradation and habitat destruction, never mind reversing it, would require a twenty-fold improvement in the environmental performance of our current technology within four decades. Even the halving of resource use, which the new Club of Rome report argues is feasible, will not, the authors warn us, be sufficient to halt global warming (*Factor Four*, 1997).

The consumer society is central to the problem, because high consumption means huge impacts. The fuels burned in industrial countries release three-quarters of the sulphur and nitrous oxides that cause acid rain and generate most of the world's hazardous chemical wastes. In 1972 the Club of Rome thought that non-renewable resources such as oil and copper would be the problem, but in fact it has turned out that the key problem is the environment's inability to absorb our wastes, its so-called 'sink functions'. Forests and oceans are an essential part of the recycling of carbon dioxide (CO_2), without which we cannot survive. Were there no human impact, the absorption and emission of CO_2 would be in equilibrium, but the pollution of the oceans and the destruction of the forests threatens this essential 'carbon accountancy', with possibly devastating effects on global climate. The World Bank's 1992 report on world development forecasts that the output of the developing countries will rise by 4 per cent between 1990 and 2030, and that of industrialized countries will triple. The Bank concludes: 'Under a simple extrapolation based upon today's practices and emissions coefficients, this would produce appalling problems of pollution and damage. Tens of millions of people would probably die each year as a result of pollutants, water shortages would become intolerable, and tropical forests and other natural habitats would be a fraction of their current size. This possibility is clear and real.' It is to this problem I now turn.

CHAPTER 3

FACTS AND VALUES

An attitude to life which seeks fulfilment in the single-minded pursuit of wealth – in short materialism – does not fit into the world, because it contains no limiting principle, while the environment in which it is placed is strictly limited.

E.F. Schumacher, *Small is Beautiful*, 1973

I have argued that there is a dialectical relationship between ethics and the social and economic structures of any society. Both affect each other in an endless interchange. No-nonsense wheelers and dealers, the movers and shakers of the corporate world, may feel that ethics, like history, is bunk. But ethics cannot be so easily sidelined for, as Ronald Engel puts it in *Ethics of Environment and Development* (1990), 'The moral values and cognitive beliefs of a culture play a crucial role in how well human societies adapt to the natural environment and what kind of political and economic relationships they maintain.' Aristotle and his successors for nearly one and a half millennia understood this perfectly, and for them it was clear that the first priority was to get your questions on the meaning and purpose of human life straight, and then your economics will come right. Part of the Great Transformation was that this order was inverted: increasingly it came to be the economy, and 'growth', which gave value to human life. The deepening of older divisions between public and private, religious and secular, ethical and economic, was part of this transformation. When David Hume, in his *Treatise of Human Nature* (1739–40), refused to draw an 'ought' from an 'is', or in other words to derive an ethical imperative from what was taken to be the nature of the world, this division was given philosophical expression. The natural world henceforth has no ethical significance whatsoever. It is just a brute, contingent fact and we can do with it what we will.

The great American liberal economist J.K. Galbraith, Fritz Schumacher with his programme for economics 'as if people mattered', and the steady-state economist Herman Daly understand economics, if not as a subdiscipline of ethics, then at least as inextricably bound up with it. Most economists, however, have insisted that economics is a science and as such has nothing to do with values. As one of the most important English economists of the twentieth century, Lionel Robbins, wrote in *An Essay on the Nature and Significance of Economic Science* (1932), 'Economics deals with ascertainable facts, ethics with valuations and obligations. . . . Between the generalizations of positive and normative studies there is a logical gulf which no ingenuity can disguise and no juxtaposition in time or space bridge over.' This distinction was specious from the start because the distinction between positive and normative science itself represents a value judgment. As Daly and Cobb note, 'The insistence on value neutrality functions more to suppress dissent about basic values than to support actual neutrality.' But specious distinctions may still be formidably powerful, and the view that ethics belongs to the realm of interpersonal relations but science to the natural world (which includes immutable laws of supply and demand) has, I shall endeavour to show, brought us to the verge of disaster. It is being increasingly recognized that what we need is not a new and better technical fix but a new ethic.

The Great Transformation was not responsible for the distinction between fact and value which we now take for granted, but it certainly immeasurably strengthened it. For earlier cultures, as we know, the earth was often regarded as sacred, and when Israel desacralized nature it nevertheless understood it as gift, an understanding institutionalized in the practice of 'grace' (giving thanks) before meals. As a gift, the earth and living creatures, what today we call the environment, were to be respected and treasured – not callously abused. Killing animals in that tradition, for example, was a 'permission' not a right, and many ancient rituals of sacrifice may have their origin in that recognition.

The slow growth in science and technology which began to gain pace in the sixteenth century bred a quite different, instrumental, attitude to nature, notoriously expressed in the words of Francis Bacon (1561–1626) as 'putting nature to the test'. Of course it is wrong to take this out of context. Bacon's world was still largely at the mercy of the environment, and the improvements in medical science and conditions of life which we take for granted arose in large part from replacing the deductive logic of scholastic thought with the empirical approach that was prepared to experiment with the living world. Today, however, the situation is quite different. Not only are there vastly many more of us, but we also have a vastly greater capacity to do harm. Bacon's world was one where the sacramental quality of life was still taken for granted. That world has been dissolved by the priority of profit, which gives us our new scale of values.

As an illustration of those values in action we can take *The Economist*'s report on the Kyoto summit on global warming on 20 December 1997. It headed its article: 'Environmental scares: Plenty of gloom in planet plenty.' It rehearsed the well-worn argument that from the days of Malthus the critics have got it wrong and we should, therefore, be sceptical about global warming as well. A month later scientists working in Antarctica announced that an ice shelf of 8000 square miles (20,700 km), the Larsen A, was about to break away from the subcontinent. The temperature at the pole is warming five times faster than elsewhere on earth, and grass is growing there. These changes could have an enormous change on weather patterns, slowing or even halting ocean currents, such as the Gulf Stream.

There are at least three problems with *The Economist*'s 'business as usual' approach. The first is that, since the earth is finite, a tiny planet in galactic terms, resources obviously cannot be infinite. It is common sense that there must be a limit to its 'carrying capacity'. If a ship is loaded above the Plimsoll line it sinks: there is an analogous danger to the earth. The question of 'throughput' – population multiplied by per capita resource use – is obviously raised as the number of consumers exponentially increase. As Daly and Cobb note, 'If "needs" include an automobile for each of a billion Chinese, then sustainable development is impossible. The whole issue of sufficiency can no longer be avoided.' Arguments then centre on what constitutes the earth's Plimsoll line, and whether some estimates, such as those of the Worldwatch Institute, are not much too cautious.

Deeper problems are bound up with the fact that conventional economics (as represented, for example, by *The Economist*) remains trapped in Isaac Newton's seventeenth-century mechanistic world view of its origins. For the eighteenth century the machine, especially the clock, was the favourite analogy for understanding the universe and human subsystems like economies. But the earth is not a machine. As the environmental scientist James Lovelock has argued, it is a little-understood organism, characterized by feedback loops which we ignore at our peril. And Newton had not discovered the second law of thermodynamics. In classical economics 'circular flow' can go on expanding infinitely. Unfortunately, as the distinguished Romanian economist Nicholas Georgescu-Roegen (1901–94) pointed out in 1971, energy degrades and entropy sets in not only in the material world but in the economy as well. Our human economies function within what the North American farmer-philosopher Wendell Berry calls 'the Great Economy', the whole ecosystem, finite and materially closed. The economy, which depends on harnessing every form of physical energy, is subject to these constraints. For the eighteenth and nineteenth centuries, says Daly (*Beyond Growth*), man-made capital was the fundamental limiting factor, but we now have to recognize that it is natural capital that is the fundamental limit.

The underlying problem, however, is ethical. From the beginning, as Homer realized, human behaviour has been characterized by hubris – the arrogant refusal to acknowledge limits. Nowhere has this been more evident than in the behaviour of technological man, as the present fascination with the *Titanic* ought to remind us. As we know, human beings are products of evolution like everything else, and the history of human cultures is the story of their slow interaction with the environment. We now know that native cultures could be as disrespectful of the environment as modern ones, but given the tiny size of the world's population (estimated at 500 million in 1650) and the limited technologies available – the harnessing of wind and water and animal traction, the use of fire for clearing forests – little impact on the earth's ecosystem was made. When development was inappropriate, as in ancient Sumer, cultures died out.

With the harnessing of fossil-fuel energy, the balance between human beings and the environment changed. Rather than a garden to till, or a force to struggle with, the environment became rather a limitless resource. Janet Abramowitz points out (Starke, ed., *State of the World 1997*) that hubris is embodied in the very way in which Gross Domestic Product (GDP) is measured, without reference to the services provided by nature. What she calls 'The world's largest biochemical R & D [Research and Development] industry' is the environment. But no price is put on this, or if it is, then it is put on it to be exploited by the big corporations.

The contradictions which follow from a fundamentally mistaken approach to the resources of the planet have generated a whole range of concrete problems to do with resources, environmental degradation and threats to the planet's ecosystem. I consider the issues under three key headings: population and resources; the macro problems of global warming and the ozone layer; and problems of environmental degradation.

Population and Resources

As we saw in the last chapter we have to set population growth and the question of resources alongside one another. No one disputes that a world which had a total population of 1.6 billion at the start of the century now has one of 5.77 billion, currently growing at 80 million per year. That this increase is less than demographers were expecting until recently is due, unfortunately, not to better birth control, or poor nations achieving an economic plateau, but to high mortality rates in areas like the former Soviet Union or sub-Saharan Africa. Most of this growth has occurred in the last forty years – world population has almost doubled since 1961. Although fertility rates show a slight fall-off, the base population rate is so large that very extensive increases are inevitable. This in turn implies huge increases in consumption.

Perhaps the most dramatic example of the way in which we are locked into the ecosystem ourselves, and not 'masters of all we survey' is our dependence on the process of photosynthesis, turning sunlight into consumable energy, in the four biological systems of forests, grasslands, fisheries and croplands. The amount of solar energy converted by photosynthesis by these systems, minus the energy they use themselves, is called Net Primary Production (NPP), the basis of all life. The *State of the World 1992* report (Starke, ed.) cites Peter Vitousek of Stanford University who calculates that 40 per cent of NPP now goes directly to human needs, a share which could double to 80 per cent within forty years given the rate of population growth. Further expansion would be impossible, he argues, because we cannot survive without the services of other species. Wilfred Beckerman, formerly Professor of Economics at London, scorns this claim, but he seems to think that what is being proposed is something arcane about photosynthesis (*Small is Stupid*, 1995). Rather, it is simply a way of insisting that human beings are dependent on their environment, including millions of other creatures, and cannot survive without it. Common sense? One would think so.

A threat to fundamental resources with which we are more familiar is the question of water. After evaporation and flood run-off, 14,000 cubic kilometres are left to be shared by the world's growing population, which obviously has less to go round each year. Not only is there less per person year by year but the greatest pressure on water is from agriculture, which has to feed the world's burgeoning population, and needs water to do so. In a review of the world's water problems in 1992 (*The Last Oasis*), Sandra Postel noted that, 'In many parts of the world, water use is nearing the limits of natural systems,' and in some areas they have been surpassed. Problems from the irresponsible use of water from age-old aquifer resources are prominent both in Arab countries, like Libya and Saudi Arabia, where they are used quite unrealistically to grow grain in the desert for a few decades, and in the United States where irrigated land in Texas, for example, has shrunk by a third. There growth in irrigation has fallen behind population growth since 1979, reducing the irrigated area per person by 7 per cent. In India and China the drilling of wells has led to sharp drops in the level of ground water, in the case of Tamil Nadu by as much as 25–30 metres (80–100 feet) in one decade. Indian cities like Delhi or Madras face drinking-water crises every year, but even in Great Britain, where the dismal weather has been the stock subject of popular humour since time immemorial, water restrictions are now chronic. The problem of limits is starker in regard to water than with any other resource. Technical fixes, like the Israeli drip-feed irrigation system, the increasing use of waste water, and improved desalination processes, can do something, but the strain on water is already well established.

Problems with water have been exacerbated by the hubris of much water technology. The best-known example of this is that of the Aral Sea, part of the former Soviet Union, which has largely dried up due to up-stream irrigation projects. Not only has a once-thriving fishing industry, and the communities it supported, been wiped out, but typhoid, hepatitis and cancer have followed in its wake. In some cases irrigation projects have contributed to the spread of water-borne diseases such as bilharzia from 10 per cent of the population to more than 80 per cent. These examples ought at least to give us pause for thought, and suggest that we are not simply free to do as we choose. Such schemes can also cause environmental devastation. In Thailand, for example, a 1965 dam project at Ubolratana led to a 50 per cent loss of forest cover in two decades.

Rivers are no respecters of the arbitrary boundaries established by human political and cultural settlements. Energy or irrigation projects upstream already lead to chronic conflict around the Nile, the Tigris and the Euphrates, while in India the states of Karnataka and Tamil Nadu squabble constantly over the waters of the Cauvery. The prospect of water wars is widely canvassed, but in fact, as some military analysts have pointed out, we have already had them, since Israel's occupation of the Golan Heights was effectively about who controls the headwaters of the Jordan.

We can turn now from water to food, and especially to grain. *The Economist's* claims, at the end of 1997, of marked progress in eliminating hunger around the world are in stark contrast to the *Oxfam Poverty*

Report 1995, which, speaking of the 'silent emergency' of poverty, alleges that, 'One in four of the world's people live in absolute want, unable to meet their basic needs. Millions more live close to this perilous condition on the very margins of survival.' Has vast progress been made in two years then? Certainly not in Papua New Guinea where in 1998 there was famine caused by drought. But perhaps the Oxfam report is nothing but scaremongering, drummed up by its directors, eager to boost their 'fame' and their salaries. . . . *The Economist* carries two World Bank graphs which differ significantly from the United States Department of Agriculture graphs for the same facts, namely the amount of world grain production per person. The scientists at the latter organization are markedly less optimistic than those at the former. It is common knowledge, easily checked, that the eleven warmest years since record-keeping began in 1866 have all occurred since 1979. This has affected grain production. Lester Brown of the Worldwatch Institute, a particular target of *The Economist* article, agrees that world grain production nearly tripled between 1950 and 1990 but then argues that it has slowed down to 0.7 per cent per year since then, which 'helps explain why carry-over stocks of grain in 1996 were at an all time low and why prices of wheat and corn set record highs'. Brown argues that much of the land pushed into grain production since 1950 is now suffering from erosion, and that a great deal of the land all round the world is disappearing under concrete as cities and highways expand. For various reasons the use of fertilizers which was partly responsible for the vast increase in grain production has also peaked. Brown's conclusion is that, 'The world's farmers face a steady shrinkage in both grainland and irrigation water per person.' In any case, it has been argued that 4–6 hectares (10–15 acres) are required to maintain the consumption of the average person living in a high income country. By 1990 only 1.7 hectares (4 acres) per capita of such land was left. It is, then, a physical impossibility for the world to consume at anything approaching North American levels.

Traditionally, grain (the staff of life) has been supplemented by fish. The world's fish catch, which in 1950 was a mere 19 million tons had by 1995 reached the staggering figure of 112 million tons, 21 million tons of which came from fish farms. The wild fish catch remains the real staple, and here the decline in fish stocks all over the world has become another well-established fact, instanced by decimated communities where once huge numbers of small boats went to sea. Both on the west coast of India and on the east coast of Britain, for example, there were fishing communities which went back millennia. In both cases overfishing has devastated them, leading to unemployment and, in India, to local starvation. In Senegal the livelihoods of over 35,000 fisherfolk are threatened by the encroachment of European Union (EU) fleets into their fishing grounds, exporting their unsustainable practices to other waters. The government welcomes them because they receive foreign exchange for fishing quotas, but this is hardly an exchange for the life of whole communities. The Oxfam report comments: 'This is the unacceptable face of trade in operation.' In the Philippines mangrove swamps have been cleared at an average rate of 3000 hectares (7500 acres) a year to make way for large commercial prawn farms for the Japanese market. The destruction of the mangroves means a progressive lowering of fish catches each year for local fisherfolk.

In the North Sea, catches of cod, whiting and herring have collapsed because the use of echo-sounders makes it too easy to catch them. In Britain disputes about fish have led to 'cod wars' and angry clashes with Spanish fishermen. Industrialized fishing methods also damage the ecosystems which support aquatic life. The problem is that the fishing industry now has more than twice the capacity to catch all the available fish. It is massively overcapitalized. As Anne Platt McGinn points out (Starke, ed., *State of the World 1998*), 'In an open-access fishery, resources are owned by no one, and the fishery is open to all comers. If one person does not catch the available fish, someone else will. As a result fishers have little incentive to conserve resources.' The Dundee *Courier* (24 January 1998) carries news of the 'virtual extinction' of some species over the past twenty years and of large numbers of mutated cod, thought to be due to the dumping of radioactive waste at sea in the '40s and '50s. In Holland fertilizers used by farmers have so contaminated fish-breeding grounds that half of the fish catch has to be thrown back into the sea because of its diseased appearance. The

UN Food and Agriculture organization reports that eleven of the world's fifteen major fishing areas and 69 per cent of the world's major fish species are in decline.

As noted above, to an increasing extent countries are turning to fish farming, but this too is not without its problems. Richard Douthwaite (*The Growth Illusion*, 1992) records the problems which arose from salmon farming in Ireland. They were fed with the small fish capelin. So many were caught that sea urchins, on whose spat they fed, multiplied out of control and consumed the seaweed beds where cod and other fish spawned. As a result the cod population crashed. Seals had to go south to search for food, and the Faroese couldn't catch their cod quota. When farmed salmon escape and mate with wild salmon the new strains cannot cope with the conditions in which the wild stock has evolved over thousands of years. And, furthermore, the farms encourage the spread of lice and infections from farmed to wild fish.

Macro Problems

So much for the problems of basic resources, but arguably more serious still are the well-publicized 'macro problems' of global warming and the loss of the ozone layer. A prominent group of scientists in the United States maintain that 'environmental scares' are either problems manufactured by environmental groups to drum up membership or, if they do signal real effects, then these are insignificant or possibly even beneficial. Thus Hugh Ellsaesser of the Lawrence Livermore National Laboratory says that, 'Carbon dioxide will exert primarily beneficial effects on the biosphere.' (See Andrew Rowell, *Green Backlash*, 1996 for an account of these scientists, and their connection with right-wing groups and fossil-fuel industries.) Geologists have also shown that huge environmental changes have happened before, and that the planet has recovered. Of course many scientists, perhaps the majority, take the contrary view. So who are we to believe? When we are told, as by Ellsaesser, that more radiation will do us good, and that exposure to the Chernobyl fallout will be a net health benefit, scepticism is suggested.

Let us take the growth in the hole in the ozone layer. The pro-growth scientists maintain that claims about this growth rest on inadequate science. Other scientists, however, have found marine plankton under stress through increased ultraviolet radiation which is a consequence of ozone loss. This could be potentially extremely serious, because plankton is the foundation of the marine ecosystem. Marine plant plankton and land plants put the oxygen into the earth's atmosphere and process carbon dioxide in photosynthesis. Douthwaite warns:

> If the growth rates of both types of plant were seriously damaged by high levels of UV radiation, not only would food supplies plunge but the green-house effect would accelerate as untreated carbon dioxide built up and prevented excess heat being radiated off into space. . . . If things ever reached this stage events would spiral out of control. The accelerated greenhouse warming would destroy much of the remaining land plants and encourage vast fires, which would not only produce even more carbon dioxide and thus speed up the warming but also increase the rate of damage to the ozone layer. There is a very real chance that the quantity of CFCs already released is enough to destroy most life forms on earth – several million tonnes of them are already swirling around in the atmosphere, gradually floating up towards the ozone layer, a journey that can take 120 years.
>
> *(The Growth Illusion, 1992)*

Now without doubt this will be dismissed by those in favour of the present economic system as typical environmental hysteria. But given the findings about plankton, should we not be a tiny bit cautious? The problem of the loss of the ozone layer is a prime example of the fact that ignorance is not bliss. As Douthwaite points out, the potential damage caused by chlorofluorocarbons is a warning to us that even seemingly harmless 'advances' can have unexpected side effects. They were invented in the 1930s as a breakthrough in the provision of cheap refrigeration, and seemed to have no side effects. It may now be the case that they have caused serious and possibly irreparable damage.

Earlier I quoted reports about the break-up of the Larsen A platform in the Antarctic, proof positive, one might think, that global warming is occurring. Something to celebrate, according to Edward Krug: it will turn the world into a Garden of Eden. This is not the view of the Commonwealth Secretariat. They accept the view that if no emission cuts are made, global mean temperature would rise by 3°F before 2100. Vegetation and forests would be affected and deserts would expand. The sea level would rise by 0.65 metres (2 feet), uprooting huge numbers of people – 10 million live within one metre of the high-tide level on the river deltas of Bangladesh, Egypt and Vietnam alone. Many small island republics would be wiped out. The Secretariat calculates that, if the sea level rises one metre, 14 per cent of Bangladesh's cropped area would be inundated, 10 per cent of the population would be displaced, and land producing 2 million tons of rice, 400,000 tons of vegetables, 200,000 tons of sugar, 100,000 tons of pulses, and accommodating 3.7 million cattle, sheep and goats and 1.9 million homes would be lost. They also note that extreme storm surges such as those which left over 138,000 people dead in 1991 would be more likely.

Richard Douthwaite points out (*The Growth Illusion*) that global warming will also affect supplies of drinking water around the world. Lakes and rivers could dry up, and it is calculated that New York could easily have only 60 per cent of the water it needs by 2050. Changes in global weather patterns are not a concern for the world's poor alone. Western insurance companies are also worried, as they have faced a huge increase in storm-related claims. Violent winds and rains seem to be on the increase. This change in weather patterns also has broader health implications – for instance, the possibility that a warmer Europe could once more be a malarial region. More serious still, Douthwaite observes, is that the earth might leave its present stable climatic regime and move to another either very much hotter or colder. The Garden of Eden? Krug works for a business lobby group known as the Committee for a Constructive Tomorrow, whose brief is to fight for economic growth. Could the fact that the biggest culprit in the 20 per cent rise above the pre-industrial level of the earth's temperature is carbon dioxide, produced by fossil-fuel consumption, deforestation and new types of land use, have anything to do with his enthusiasm for global warming?

The world's consumer class is responsible for an estimated two-thirds of carbon dioxide emissions. The poor release one-tenth of a ton each year per person; the middle-income group half a ton; the consumer class three and a half tons; the richest tenth of Americans eleven tons. Even to stabilize greenhouse gas emissions requires a cut of a billion tons in today's output, and the burden naturally falls on the heaviest producers, the rich countries. One can see why pro-growth lobbies need to pour scorn on these projections. On present-day figures it is possible to calculate an emissions allowance for every person on earth, given the capacity of global 'sinks' – the inbuilt mechanisms for dealing with potentially toxic wastes. In *The Growth Illusion* (1992), Douthwaite writes: 'When one remembers that the average family car covering 11,000 miles [18,000 km] a year burns at least two persons' fossil-fuel allowance and heating an average British house takes four persons' allowances one can see that cuts of the size needed are going to hit so close to home that it is impossible to see politicians taking the initiative and making them: only tremendous public pressure or a desperate crisis will get them to act.'

These concerns led to the world summit in Kyoto at the end of 1997 which met to address the issue. In a discussion which nearly ended without agreement it was decided that high-polluting countries such as the United States could trade their pollution by making payments to countries that pollute less, thus averaging out world-wide pollution. Reporting perspectives on it make interesting reading. The *Guardian* reported that the Kyoto deal 'leaves the US free to pollute'. The *Washington Post* commented: 'The European Union's acceptance, after years of scepticism, of the idea of market mechanisms . . . represents significant progress.' *Le Monde* was the only paper which raised the question of justice: 'The message of Kyoto is that our societies should stop basing their growth on the principle of an interminable scramble to consume more energy, and that since they will have to make do with less they should strive to be more effective.' It notes the introduction of a pollution market, but then comments that:

> There would be an intolerable perversion of the system if that market were to become a channel through which the rich, because they were rich, could

simply buy from the poor the right to go on behaving wastefully. It would be rather as if certain car owners were allowed to buy the right to drive at 200 kph [125 mph] while all other drivers were forced to observe the speed limit in the general interest.

The Economist, meanwhile, is naturally sceptical. It underlines the fact that scientists are 'almost unanimous' about the phenomenon. Let us go on growing, then, until we are certain. As Mishan remarked, people who throw themselves off a ninety-storey building are conscious until they reach the first floor. By then it is too late to change their minds.

Environmental Degradation

A third set of problems is bound up with environmental degradation of many kinds. In the West we are familiar with the erosion of the countryside, the pollution of rivers with chemical wastes, regular emergencies following from oil spills off our coasts, sewage off, and sometimes on, our beaches, and the destruction of wildlife through pesticides. Elsewhere in the world there have been a number of terrible industrial accidents, the worst in 1986 at the nuclear power station at Chernobyl whose core went into meltdown, the effects of which will last for centuries. We do not always realize, however, how large-scale the threat to the environment is.

We can begin with the world's forests because again, without them we cannot survive, as they process carbon dioxide and function as 'the lungs of the world'. The Economist mocks the series of 'scares' of recent times: 'In the early 1980s acid rain became the favourite cause of doom. Lurid reports appeared of widespread forest decline in Germany. . . . What happened? [The forests] recovered. The biomass stock of European forests actually increased during the 1980s. . . . Forests did not decline: they thrived.' This is not the view of the United Nations Human Development Report 1997 which notes that, 'World air pollution is devastating Europe's forests, causing economic losses of $35 billion a year.' Janet Abramowitz, in the State of the World 1998 report, writes, 'Serious declines in forest quality are affecting much of the world's forests . . . more than a quarter of Europe's trees show moderate to severe defoliation [from the stresses of atmospheric pollution].' And if in Europe and the United States the amount of tree cover has increased slightly, nevertheless worldwide we are losing 11.3 million hectares [28 million acres] of forest annually, and the loss of tropical forest is especially great. The link to the world economic system is shown by the fact that it is some of the world's most indebted countries, Brazil, Mexico and Zaire, which, together with Bolivia, Indonesia, Malaysia and Venezuela are responsible for half of the tropical forest lost between 1991 and 1995. Consumption of paper is increasing more than any other forest product, and, according to Abramowitz, two-thirds of it is made from virgin forest. The destruction of forests has massive implications for the world's climate, and in addition leads to soil erosion, flooding, siltation and loss of productive land. Why is this happening? As Michael Redclift notes of the Amazon basin, 'Energy consumption in Brazil . . . is linked to an economic model that places economic profitability at the level of the world system above the conservation of a global resource. A global sink is being destroyed in the interests of Brazil's global integration within markets for minerals and bauxite.' (*Wasted*, 1996.)

In Costa Rica the expansion of beef exports to the North American market was a driving force in the country's trade expansion during the '60s and '70s. The real cost of this, however, has been the destruction of the country's rainforest, only 17 per cent of which remained intact by the mid 1980s. In the Philippines commercial logging removed 10 million cubic metres (350 million cubic feet) of timber annually in the 1970s. By the end of the 1980s the country was beginning to import wood. In Thailand where logging reduced forest cover from 55 per cent to 28 per cent of the country's land area between the 1960s and 1988, deforestation contributed to mud slides, floods and consequent loss of life. When the Thai government banned logging, the companies moved to Cambodia where 2 million hectares (5 million acres) have already been destroyed.

The destruction of forests, particularly in the South, contributes hugely to the loss of biodiversity, which in turn has implications for medicine. The background rate of extinctions in the course of evolution is estimated at three species per year. This has now risen to at least 1000 species per year. (*State of the World 1998.*) Biodiversity is threatened by 'development' which replaces rich and varied natural habitats by monocultures for commercial exploitation. The 'green revolution' of the 1960s and '70s replaced the wide variety of indigenous varieties with monocultures, which may then be susceptible to disease. A third of the plants that grew in the Netherlands at the start of the century have become extinct. Insects and other animals have disappeared along with the plants. Areas such as swamps and wetlands were viewed in development ideology as wasted land, productive only if drained or filled. 'Today', says Abramowitz (*State of the World 1997*), 'their roles in cleansing water, recycling nutrients, recharging aquifers, controlling floods, and supporting productive sources, such as fish, wildlife and wild produce, are being recognized . . . so is their ability to protect coasts from storms.' But more than a quarter of the coastal wetlands in Europe and the USA have been lost, and perhaps more in other parts of the world. Plants cannot survive without pollination, but many of the species which provide this indispensable work are threatened by extinction through pesticides or the destruction of their native habitat. The same is true of nature's own pest control services, such as frogs. The preservation of biodiversity, the Worldwatch team note (*State of the World 1998*), rests on how well sustainable approaches to forestry, agriculture, livestock husbandry, river management and other land uses are created. It is primarily a cultural and political matter. 'Ultimately it means replacing our consumer culture with a less materialist and far more environmentally literate way of life.'

Another area of both hubris and of highly publicized disagreement is in the nuclear industry. The UK Atomic Energy Authority (UKAEA) renamed Windscale 'Sellafield' after an accident there. In a high cost publicity exercise it has spent decades reassuring everyone that nuclear energy is perfectly safe. An official enquiry in 1997 found that unusual clusters of child cancer in the area around the plant had 'nothing to do with Sellafield'. Meanwhile Norway is now detecting an eightfold increase in radioactive waste reaching its shores, and traces this to Sellafield, while lobsters caught in the area are 32 times over the limit the European Union deems fit for human consumption. The Authority claims that after years of secrecy it is adopting a stance of openness, but only six months previously statements that thousands of drums dumped off the Channel Islands contained no plutonium 'were exposed as shameless lies'. The environmental journalist George Monbiot writing in the *Guardian* (10 December 1997) comments, 'UKAEA's advertised change of heart merits as much suspicion as any of its other public pronouncements.'

Other forms of pollution naturally grow with economic expansion. The OECD (Organization for Economic Co-operation and Development) countries generated 303 billion tons of hazardous waste in 1990. As other economies grow, so will the waste, while problems of disposing with it still prove intractable. The growth in the world automobile fleet will lead to further carbon dioxide emissions and greater urban pollution. Redclift reports (*Wasted*, 1996) that the amount of sulphur dioxide, nitrogen dioxide and suspended particulates, some of the most dangerous pollutants, increased by a factor of ten in Thailand, eight in the Philippines and five in Indonesia between 1975 and 1988. Five of the world's most polluted cities are now in Asia. Problems with pollution do not just mean unpleasant conditions for those forced to live in affected areas but often have serious effects on much wider ecosystems. We need to learn to respect the earth as an organism, to respect the limits of the planet's natural processes of regeneration and recycling, and its ability to deal with the toxins we generate.

The Alternative Ethic

What all these statistics illustrate beyond a doubt is that fact and value belong together, and that not only can we derive an 'ought' from an 'is', but we can also derive a categorical imperative from the way things are. The facts warn us, as Durning puts it (*How Much is Enough?*), that 'if we attempt to preserve the consumer economy indefinitely ecological forces will dismantle it savagely'.

To enable the about-turn that is called for, it is increasingly recognized that we need a new ethic. A report of various conservation groups in 1980 (*World Conservation Strategy*, 1980) noted that, 'A new ethic, embracing plants and animals as well as people, is required for human societies to live in harmony with the natural world on which they depend for their survival and well-being.' Seven years later the World Commission on Environment and Development's report, *Our Common Future*, likewise called for a 'new ethic' to underwrite sustainable development. Through the Green Movement this ethic has gained considerable ground. Michael Northcote has pointed out (*The Environment and Christian Ethics*, 1996) that to a large extent the frameworks of these reports remain utilitarian, and so tied to cost-benefit analysis. Early this century it was Martin Buber, in his seminal work *I and Thou* (1922), who mounted one of the sharpest challenges to the bureaucratic instrumentalism of his contemporary Max Weber:

> When I observe a tree, I can of course treat it as an object, quantify it, consider how much paper or furniture or how many toothpicks I can get from it. But it can also happen, if will and grace are joined, that as I contemplate the tree I am drawn into a relation, and the tree ceases to be an It. . . . What I encounter is neither the soul of a tree nor a dryad, but the tree itself.

What Buber was after was an understanding of reality as centred on relationship from which the 'natural world' was not excluded. It was an extraordinary precursor of what is today called 'environmental ethics', but is in fact better understood as an ethic of relationship, in which the virtues of justice, compassion and prudence extend beyond the social to the whole non-human world. Daly and Cobb observe that the danger is that the pleasures of the consumer culture, part of a systemically unjust world order, 'will replace the collective biophysical wisdom accumulated in the gene pool over millions of years of experience'. That wisdom taught the danger of presumption, and the need for patience, modesty and respect for the earth. The growth economy, however, is driven by hubris, by an arrogant presumption that we possess knowledge that we do not in fact have, and by a fatally flawed understanding of the economy and its relation to the environment. And as the Greek tragedians knew, hubris can destroy us.

CHAPTER 4

NORTH AND SOUTH

Without being radical or overly bold, I will tell you that the Third World War has already started – a silent war, not for that reason any the less sinister. This war is tearing down Brazil, Latin America and practically all the Third World. Instead of soldiers dying there are children, instead of millions of wounded there are millions of unemployed; instead of destruction of bridges there is the tearing down of factories, schools, hospitals and entire economies. . . . It is a war by the United States against the Latin American continent and the Third World. It is a war over the foreign debt, one which has as its main weapon interest, a weapon more deadly than the atom bomb. . . .

Luis Ignacio Silva ('Lula'), Brazilian Labour leader, 1985

In September 1997, just prior to the crisis in the so-called Tiger economies of East Asia, Oxfam published a position paper entitled 'Growth with Equity: An Agenda for Poverty Reduction'. They observed that over the past three decades East Asia had experienced the most rapid and sustained growth this century, and that this was accompanied by a silent revolution in poverty reduction. 'More people have moved out of poverty more quickly than at any time in history.' Their message was that countries serious about growth need to begin with poverty reduction and human development.

The paper goes on to acknowledge the human rights abuses, which are considerable throughout the region and horrific in places, and the devastation of forests which has represented (my comment, not theirs) not 'sustained growth' but growth that is completely unsustainable. It is fair to point out that other estimates of these economies are very different. A group from the Transnational Institute (Cavanagh, et al., *Beyond Bretton Woods*, 1994) expressed extreme caution with regard to any triumphalism, noted the Korean strikes of the late '80s, 'after decades of systematic exploitation', and the Taiwanese landscape, 'littered with poisoned soil and toxic water'. Walden Bello (*Dark Victory*, 1994) notes that the success of these economies has also much to do with the injection of huge amounts of Japanese capital. He reckons the 'elimination' of poverty in Indonesia is more statistical than real, referring to it ironically as 'one of the great mysteries of our time', a view which seems to be presently vindicated. The journalist John Pilger, meanwhile, who has seen more of the Asian 'success' at first hand than most economists, ascribes it to the 'restoration of rapacious capitalism's modern essentials – centralized state power and a rigged "market".' (*Hidden Agendas*.)

How does one balance the gains mentioned by Oxfam against the democratic deficit, the suppression of minority groups, and irreversible environmental devastation? Despite the crash of 1997 and the need for IMF support, do not the achievements of the Tiger economies once and for all establish that what John Gray called in 1992 'the benign incentives provided by the disciplines of market competition' are the way forward for the human race? (*The Moral Foundations of Market Institutions*.) The conclusions of the *United Nations Human Development Report 1997* suggests scepticism, noting that the human development index declined in 1996–97 in over thirty countries. 'The share of the poorest 20 per cent of the world's people in global income now stands at a miserable 1.1 per cent, down from 1.4 per cent in 1991 and 2.3 per cent in 1960. It continues to shrink.' Is this a temporary blip in the behaviour of benign market incentives, or is it a structural failure, like that of the Soviet command economies, which failed to understand the need for such incentives?

The debate about world debt has familiarized people with the origins of the Bretton Woods institutions – the International Monetary Fund (IMF) and the World Bank – which were set up after the Second World War to restore the war-damaged economies of the world. The idea of these institutions was to make available cash for development and restoration on terms which would 'not be destructive of national prosperity'. What remains less well known is that John

Maynard Keynes, who was the leading figure at the Bretton Woods conference, wanted to charge interest not just on countries with debts but also on those with surpluses in order to increase equality in the world market-place. This proposal was never implemented. What further militated against the attaining of parity between nations was that the IMF was not, like the United Nations, constituted democratically. Its funds for granting loans were supplied by quotas, 20 per cent of which lie with the United States, and 54 per cent with the ten richest industrialized countries. These countries therefore call the shots in making development aid available.

In the early years of the Bretton Woods institutions the world was divided into four. There were the war-torn economies of Europe and Japan which needed to be restored; there were the Communist economies which were the enemy; there was the world's leading economy, the United States; and there were the 'underdeveloped' economies of what we now call the Third World or the South. All of these groups believed in the importance of economic growth, though there were different views as to how it should be achieved. Virtually the only person who had significantly different ideas on the issue was Gandhi, and as far as economists were concerned his ideas counted for nothing. Gandhi's fellow leader in the struggle for the independence of India, Jawaharlal Nehru, believed that increasing India's heavy industry was the only way forward, and in this he was followed by most leaders in the post-colonial world. Economic growth, everyone was sure, was the route to a brighter human future. Fifty years later, basic indicators are worsening all over the Third World and the gap between rich and poor nations is bigger than ever. In terms of the now well-known UN *Human Development Report 1992* diagram, by 1992, 20 per cent of the world's people who live in the richest countries received 82.7 per cent of the world's income, while only 1.4 per cent went to the 20 per cent of the world's population in the poorest countries. The *Human Development Report 1997* shows that in 1950, before the development process, the ratio between rich and poor was that the top 20 per cent had 30 times more than the bottom 20 per cent. They now have sixty times more. In 1850 today's rich countries accounted for 35 per cent of the world's total income. By the 1980s they accounted for 68 per cent. The difference between the per capita incomes of poor and rich countries increased from 70 per cent in 1850 to more than 1000 per cent in the 1980s. Between 1989 and 1996 the number of billionaires increased from 157 to 447. The net wealth of the ten richest is one and a half the times the total national income of all the least developed nations, and the wealth of the richest Mexican equal to the combined income of 17 million of the poorest of his fellow citizens. A triumph of benign market incentives indeed! The same report comments: 'A rising tide of wealth is supposed to lift all boats. But some are more seaworthy than others. The yachts and ocean liners are indeed rising in response to new opportunities, but the rafts and rowboats are taking on water – and some are sinking fast.'

The Debt Collectors

One of the most crippling problems for the countries of the South is the question of debt. Before exploring that, it is worth reminding ourselves that paying interest on debt, which makes a handsome profit for banks, has not always been an axiom, and we have to ask how interest rates are arrived at. It seems reasonable to protect money loaned against inflation, but what is the justification for continuing to collect interest when the amount originally advanced as principal has long ago been repaid? A fair interest rate, Douthwaite remarks *(Short Circuit*, 1996), should reward the lender for the risk of making a loan, compensate for loss of purchasing power, and share between borrower and lender the benefits which flow from the way the money is used. On these criteria, the interest rates that are crippling Southern countries are deeply unjust, for they have repaid initial loans many times over. Frederick Soddy made a distinction between wealth, which has limits, and debt, which does not. Daly comments:

> Debt can endure forever; wealth cannot. . . . The positive feedback of compound interest must be offset by counteracting forces of debt repudiation, such as inflation, bankruptcy, or confiscatory taxation, all of which breed violence. Conventional wisdom considers the latter processes pathological,

but accepts compound interest as normal. Logic demands, however, that we either constrain compound interest in some way, or accept as normal and necessary one or more of the counteracting mechanisms of debt repudiation.

(*Beyond Growth*, 1996)

The fact that debt can 'endure forever' is one of the reasons that many traditional societies, and Muslim countries, still do not allow interest. U. Chapra, the Muslim economist, in *Towards a Just Monetary System* (1985), has made the case that an interest-free economy would be more efficient and lead to greater economic stability. From a more conventional standpoint Daly raises the question of what counts as 'normal'. Why should we count compound interest as 'normal' and not debt repudiation? Who establishes normality here?

Debt is a fundamental fact of our present financial world, the real motor of the world economy. Banks in fact create money by allowing people to borrow way beyond their own reserves (Rowbotham, *The Grip of Death*, 1998). The present crisis of the Southern countries, however, goes back to the formation of OPEC (Organization of Petroleum Exporting Countries) in 1973 and the rise in oil prices. The OPEC countries deposited their new oil wealth in Western banks. Since idle money loses against inflation, the banks needed to find countries to take loans. Keynes believed that interest rises should not be subject to the play of market forces, but fixed by governments; to keep interest rates stable, the IMF was to establish fixed exchange rates. In the early 1970s the fixed exchange rate collapsed, and interest rates had to be used to stabilize exchange rates. Interest rates leapt in the 1980s in response to trade and budget deficits in the United States. Export markets were hit. As export earnings fell, debt repayment obligations rose, leaving much of Africa and Latin America in a state of financial bankruptcy. In the recession the price of raw materials, on which Southern economies depend, collapsed. Debts incurred were so large that they needed new loans to finance them. In this situation the Bretton Woods institutions took on a new role. Instead of helping poorer nations, these nations were paying huge sums to the institutions. The *Oxfam Poverty Report 1995* notes that instead of calling for debt write-off, as their original charter would have indicated, 'They devoted themselves to maintaining creditor claims, in effect acting as debt collectors in indigent states. The preferred solution to the debt crisis was to divert resources on a scale bound to destroy growth and orderly adjustment.'

Between 1982 and 1990 $927 billion was advanced to the South but $1345 billion was remitted in debt service alone from Southern countries. With principal, this amounted to $12 billion 450 million per month. 'Not since the conquistadores plundered Latin America', said Morris Miller, a former employee of the World Bank, 'has the world experienced a [financial] flow in the direction we see today.' The debtor countries began the 1990s 61 per cent more in debt than they were in 1982. Sub-Saharan Africa's debt increased by 113 per cent in this period. By 1997 the debt of 41 highly indebted countries stands at $215 billion, up from $183 billion in 1990. When the question of debt remission has been raised, Western bankers have shrieked about 'moral hazard' – failing to honour debts, after all, would mean attacking the very foundations of the capitalist system. But, as the Centre for Economic Policy Research has argued ('European Economic Perspectives', March 1998), moral hazard cuts both ways. Overborrowing is overlending, and creditors, too, have to take their share of the cost of mistakes. This objection has yet to cut any ice in the debate about debt.

To meet the debt emergency the 'Brady Initiative' was introduced, a form of debt re-scheduling provided by the World Bank. Still debt repayments accounted for about one-third of export earnings and more in the very poorest countries, such as sub-Saharan Africa. Multilateral debt accounted for almost half of total debt service payments for over thirty low-income countries. Under pressure from both the indebted countries and non-governmental organizations (NGOs), the Highly Indebted Poor Countries (HIPC) initiative was adopted by the IMF and the World Bank in September 1996. This extended to all categories of debt, and established the principle that ability to pay should be the central principle guiding debt-relief operations. The criterion was compliance with two three-year IMF programmes. Unfortunately, the political will for implementation has been lacking. Germany, Japan, Italy and the United States have all acted to delay implementation and minimize the level of debt relief provided. In a scathing attack Oxfam has this to say about the IMF in a briefing on 'Poor Country Debt Relief':

> For its part, the IMF has played a highly destructive role. Two years ago, the IMF denied the existence of a debt problem and ruled out participation in any debt reduction. Today, the Fund's management and technical staff are developing foot-dragging on implementation into an art form. . . . One of the primary concerns of the Fund has been to minimize the costs to itself of financing debt relief, placing narrow institutional self-interest over the needs of the world's poorest countries. This is a scandalous abuse of power and authority.

By 1997 two countries had met the required conditions, Uganda and Bolivia. In both cases the Boards of the IMF and the World Bank chose to delay action. Uganda has the third highest child-mortality rate in Africa and one of the world's highest maternal-mortality rates. In recent years per capita spending on debt has been more than three times higher than spending on health. In Uganda's case a year's delay means that it loses $193 million in relief from debt servicing. This money amounts to six times total government spending on health or double the projected spending on education. In the same briefing Oxfam comment that the Bretton Woods institutions 'chose to place their debt-servicing claims above the interests of Uganda's poor'.

In Bolivia's case debt absorbs a quarter of government revenues, and per capita public spending on health and education is a third lower than in 1980. A year's delay costs the country $241m, more than the entire health budget and 17 times the allocation for investment in basic sanitation.

Delays to the implementation of the HIPC scheme are projected for many of the affected countries. For 24 out of the 30 HIPC countries debt repayments account for more than 20 per cent of government revenues. In seven, public spending on debt is greater than public spending on health and education combined. Oxfam comment, 'For countries rooted near the bottom of the world's human welfare league, this is an intolerable situation.' Allowing debt to destroy the growing minds and bodies of young children and to undermine communities is the antithesis of civilized behaviour. 'Nothing can justify it – and it should not be tolerated.' And yet, in May 1998 at the Birmingham meeting of the leading seven industrial nations and Russia (the so-called 'G8' group), this is just what we saw once again. Eligible countries were 'urged to take the policy measures needed' to reduce debt – in other words to adopt the monetarist conditions imposed by the IMF. This amounts quite simply to putting the blame on the poor and business as usual (*Guardian*, 18 May 1998). The refusal to remit debt is about the maintenance of the world financial system, and the profitability of banks, built on the whole abstract system of interest.

In Oxfam's view the imposition of a six-year, as opposed to three-year conditionality has no obvious reason, 'unless the aim is to extend the policy influence of the IMF'. This is a serious problem given what they speak of as the Fund's 'combination of short-term monetarism and indifference to social outcomes'.

Again, this needs to be put in context. Lester Thurow reported that at a world economics conference in 1982, 'The intellectual disarray was complete – no shared ideas about what was going on, why, and what could be done about our ailing economies.' Disputes in economics today are like those in medieval theology, with different schools anathematizing each other, but with no obvious indicators of who is right or wrong. Unfortunately it is not now a few heretics who stand to be burned, but whole communities and the environment devastated, in the interest of a super-rich financial ruling class. It is important to remember the disagreement amongst economists because, as the Oxfam position paper on debt relief makes clear, monetarism is still a reigning orthodoxy at the IMF which adversely affects the lives of millions of people. Academic economists will at once insist that monetarist orthodoxy died in the '80s, but let them explain how else to describe the nostrums which guide the application of the 'structural adjustment programmes' (SAPs). A six-year commitment to such programmes is needed to qualify for the HIPC scheme. These involve the abolition or easing of exchange and import controls, devaluation of the local currency, cuts to public spending, high interest rates and pegging wages. These conditions are insisted on with fundamentalist fervour. Writing of Mozambique in 1996, Jeffrey Sachs, of the Harvard Institute for International Development, said: 'While moderate to low inflation is an important ingredient for long-term economic growth, reconstruction and rapid growth in Mozambique should take precedence over a rapid disinflation.' He was prepared to allow inflation targets of 20–35 per cent for 1996–97, but of course this would conflict with IMF orthodoxy (Oxfam, 'Debt Relief for Mozambique', 1997). Thurow commented in 1983 (in *Dangerous Currents*) that, 'Accepting the conventional supply-demand model of the economy is rather like believing that the world is flat, or that the sun revolves round the earth – you can make a rigorous case, on paper, for both propositions, but hard evidence is more than a bit scarce.' If you act according to these beliefs, he added, you get into a lot of trouble.

This is indeed what has happened. The impact of 'structural adjustment programmes' on the debtor countries has been catastrophic, as the *Oxfam Poverty Report 1995* points out: 'Increasing unemployment, declining real wages, and reduced social welfare provision have been almost universal features of structural adjustment.' The report gives many examples to substantiate its case. In Zimbabwe the cost of food increased by 50 per cent while wages fell far below inflation. In Peru food prices rose by 2500 per cent in a year and the number of people in extreme poverty soared. All over the South, spending on education fell and continues to fall, with critical implications for the future of these countries. The Oxfam report shows how, in country after country, expenditure on debt is crippling programmes to help the poor. In Tanzania, for example, they report that health and educational systems are crumbling: 'Real spending per primary school child is one-third lower than it was in the early 1980s. . . . Illiteracy rates have increased from 10 per cent to 15 per cent since 1986.' Such conditions are likely to continue while the country has to spend four times as much on debt servicing as it does on health and education. In Niger, the world's poorest country, for every $1 spent on health and education, $3 are spent on debt servicing. In short, from the perspective of the South, SAPs have been a disaster, and have done next to nothing to help these economies. But, comments Walden Bello (*Dark Victory*, 1994), 'Judged by its underlying strategic goals of shoring up the interests of the North and resubordinating the South within a North-dominated international economic system, structural adjustment has undoubtedly been a tremendous success.' He argues that IMF policies are only part of a programme of the resubordination of the South, driven by the dismay of right-wing think-tanks like the Heritage Foundation at the clamour for a 'New International Economic Order' in the 1970s. They apparently regarded this demand as an assault on free-market values.

Again, to put this in another context, were the HIPC initiative implemented, it would cost over an eight-year period less than United States citizens spend annually on sports shoes. In its paper on debt relief, Oxfam comment: 'Enlarging the budgetary provision to finance an initiative capable of making an important contribution to poverty reduction is not beyond the financial means of the industrialized countries. The question is whether or not it is beyond their capacity for political action.' On most understandings this might be taken to be a question of justice. But then, talk of justice confuses the issue: what is important is the good life – for some.

Industries which are targeted for expansion because they increase exports and make the economy 'healthier', are often inappropriate and involve dangers to health for ordinary people. In Zimbabwe, for instance, structural adjustment has focused on horticulture, flowers, tobacco and cotton. This strategy will generate some employment, the *Oxfam Poverty Report 1995* comments, '. . . but it will do little to enhance the autonomy or reduce the vulnerability of the poorest sections of society'. Agricultural production does not grow but falls in countries sticking closest to the adjustment programmes, with damaging consequences for rural employment, poverty reduction and food self-reliance. In many countries the ten-hour day has been reintroduced, with longer hours at peak periods, no sick pay, safety standards or labour rights. In the Philippines workers who produce Nike shoes, which sell from $73 to $135 in the West, are paid as little as

15 cents per hour to produce them. There are no unions and overtime is often mandatory.

Countries which refused to toe the monetarist line have been severely disciplined and the availability of IMF loans has been heavily politically biased. For example, in the early '70s Allende's Socialist Chile was refused a loan made freely available to the Fascist Pinochet regime immediately afterwards. Socialist Vietnam was refused one, but South Africa was granted one almost equal to its increase in military spending immediately after the Soweto riots in 1976. The Somoza regime in Nicaragua was granted one, the Sandanista was not. The US Treasury Secretary of the time, Donald Regan, commented, 'The IMF is essentially a non-political institution. . . . But this does not mean that United States' political and security interests are not served by the IMF.' (George, *A Fate Worse than Debt*, 1988.) In the '80s the extraordinarily repressive regime in El Salvador was given standby credit in which normal IMF conditions on interest rates, subsidies and the prices of agricultural goods were ignored. In 1995, according to an Oxfam briefing, an IMF spokesman in Mozambique noted an unprogrammed expansion in the money supply and condemned the increase in the industrial minimum wage from about $15 to $20 per month. The country was warned that its programme might be considered 'off track' and the special loan facilities were in fact 'lapsed' for a few months, presumably as a shot over the bows. A study of IMF policy concludes that it 'intervenes massively in the economic, social and political structures of deficit countries' (Körner, et al., *The IMF and the Debt Crisis*, 1986).

When is Free Trade not Free Trade?

Classical economic theory, as elaborated by Adam Smith, saw trade as 'an engine of growth' through the theory of comparative advantage – namely that countries are able to trade with one another, exchanging the goods in which each specialize. Even in Smith's lifetime this did not work, as Britain found the need in the 1760s and '70s to restrict Bengal's muslin trade to benefit its own cloth industry. The theory ignores the question of unequal power and technological knowledge.

At Bretton Woods in 1944 Keynes proposed a third body, an international trading organization, to regulate world trade and work for parity. This was not put into practice because of opposition from the United States, and for fifty years its place was taken by the General Agreement on Tariffs and Trade (GATT), until the formation of the World Trade Organization (WTO) in 1994. Both GATT and now the WTO have been effectively an arm of the Organization for Economic Co-operation and Development (OECD), a rich nations' club. The results of their policies are that real commodity prices were 45 per cent lower in the 1990s than in the 1980s and that terms of trade for the least developed countries have declined by a cumulative 50 per cent over the past quarter century. This is set to continue: two-thirds of the benefits of the 1994 agreement will go to industrialized countries, and above all to the European Union, while Africa and the Caribbean stand to lose.

From the beginning, a double standard has characterized the GATT commitment to 'free' trade. This dogma has been used as a stick to beat the weak, but has been ignored by the strong. Thus an article in *The World Economy* in 1986 noted that, 'The breakdown in the GATT system is nowhere more evident than in trade relations between developed and developing countries. Here an undeclared trade war is in progress.' (Singer and Ansari, *Rich and Poor Countries*, 1988.) In the '80s products subject to restriction climbed from 20 to 30 per cent in the US. Four hundred trade bills designed to prevent imports and protect home products were introduced in the US Congress in 1985 alone (George, *A Fate Worse than Debt*, 1988). The European Union specifically excluded the three principal Southern exports – metals, agricultural products and textiles – from the scheme. 'Non-tariff barriers' are erected against Southern products. One-fifth of all non-fuel exports from developing countries are now covered by these, of which the multi-fibre arrangement (MFA) is the most notorious. Its purpose is to protect the textile industries of the North against cheap imports from the South, and it will remain in force until 2005. As Oxfam point out in their *Poverty Report 1995*, 'The overall cost of the MFA to developing countries has been estimated at around $50bn a year: roughly equal to the total flow of development assistance provided by Northern

Governments.' The UN *Human Development Report 1997* points out that the 48 least-developed countries now account for less than 0.3 per cent of world trade – half the level of two decades ago. These countries are now being by-passed by private capital transfers, which have displaced aid as the main channel for North–South financial flows. This pattern of distribution is not accidental, they comment. It is a direct result of the rules governing world trade and investment, which are created to further the interests of the wealthy countries. The issues of debt and primary commodities were conspicuous by their absence on the agenda of the Uruguay Round, unlike intellectual property rights and trade-related investment, a measure of rich country dominance of the proceedings (*Partnership 2000: European Solidarity Towards Equal Participation of People, Proposals on Trade and Investment,* May 1997).

As Charles Elliott writes in his book, *Comfortable Compassion* (1987), terms of trade are inherently biased against the South because there cannot be competition between the commodity exports of the South and the manufactured goods of the rich nations. Demand for commodities grows only slowly and competition increases; they are sold on the market, whereas tractors and turbines are sold on a cost plus basis. Between 1980 and 1993 prices for primary commodities fell by more than half in relation to prices for manufactured goods. According to the Oxfam report of 1995, 'The estimated annual loss to developing countries over this period was around $100bn: more than twice the total flow of aid in 1990.' This amounts again to a poor person's gift to the rich. One of the reasons for the decline in primary commodity prices is overproduction and dumping by the industrialized countries, for instance of sugar by the EU. Furthermore, these countries can be caught in the market trap. Thus when Ghana increased its export of cocoa, the price fell, with the result that while it doubled its exports it saw its foreign exchange earnings fall. In Mexico subscription to the North American Free Trade Agreement spells disaster for small farmers who cannot compete with subsidized United States agriculture. The agricultural settlement of the Uruguay Round spells the same for most Southern countries. Under this agreement the Minimum Access Volume Arrangement frees up the volume of imports allowed. Because of the farm subsidy system operative in the North, this will spell disaster to farmers in the poorer nations. Each US farmer receives in subsidies roughly one hundred times the income of a corn farmer in the Philippines. Oxfam comment, 'In the real world, as distinct from the imaginary one inhabited by free traders, survival in agricultural markets depends less upon comparative advantage than upon comparative access to subsidies.' The Uruguay Round agreement, Oxfam remark, bears all the hallmarks of an elaborate act of fraud (1996 position paper on trade liberalization in the Philippines). It requires developing countries to open their food markets in the name of free-market principles while allowing the US and the EU to continue to subsidize exports.

Bello has documented the extraordinary US assault on Korean trade. Korean goods were the subject of anti-dumping measures and fierce trade legislation on the grounds that Korea engaged in unfair trade. A Korean comic which urged people to buy Korean goods provoked a hysterical reaction from a US Trade Representative, who condemned its 'outrageous rhetoric'. The result? 'Korea is now the third largest importer of US agricultural products. . . . On a per capita basis, Korea now consumes more US farm products than any other foreign nation.' (*Dark Victory*, 1994.) Similar treatment has been meted out to Indonesia, Thailand and Taiwan. More than half the allegations of unfair trade have been directed at Southern countries.

The Oxfam report of 1995 comments that, though trade has led to growth, 'It is also clear that unrestrained free trade is no longer justifiable, if it ever was, as an end in itself. Trade which is built on the foundations of unacceptable levels of social exploitation, which destroys the environments of vulnerable communities, or causes global ecological damage and disregards our obligations to future generations is not conducive to sustainable development.' But, as we have seen, this 'free trade', like the 'free' trade on which the British Empire was built, is not free at all, but rigged. It amounts to global thuggery, in which the rich countries use their financial muscle to club those already on the ground and impoverish them still further.

In the debate about growth in the most impoverished countries a number of issues are clear. First, the IMF model maintains that what benefits the poorer nations is increased consumption of their goods by the wealthier countries. More effective rules for world trade would be more to the point. Secondly, much export-led growth has proved disastrous, and done damage to sustainable local agriculture, producing poverty and famine where there was previously subsistence – this is Vandana Shiva's argument. What is needed is what the 1997 Human Development Programme calls 'pro poor growth', which concentrates on labour-using and employment-generating measures and promotes equity, for, as they comment, 'inequality usually hinders growth'. Thirdly, as Daly points out, if the standard of living enjoyed by the North cannot be generalized, then the issue of consumption has to be addressed by the wealthy nations. Oxfam remark (*Poverty Report 1995*) that two-thirds of the world's population will not reconcile itself to a level of living that is permanently diminishing in contrast to the standards enjoyed by the privileged citizens of Northern America, Europe and the oil-rich countries. Quite so. But if it is true that the world's ecology will not enable those standards to be attained by nearly 6 billion (the present figure), or 8 billion or more, the only just answer, and the only answer which can avoid a global conflagration, is to arrive at parity. The fulfilment of 'satiable needs' for the South and some other kind of needs for the North, which is what Gray's arguments for the morality of the market amount to on the macro scale, will not do. He acknowledges that a society in which the poor lack dignity, and those struck by catastrophe are left to their own devices, is not worth living in, but this is exactly the world order that the magic of the market has delivered to us.

Sooner or later the costs of injustice always make themselves felt. Some of them have been documented by Susan George in *The Debt Boomerang* (1992). In 1979, 19,000 hectares (47,000 acres) in Peru were planted to coca. As the country's debt grew, this increased tenfold. The drug problem in the Western world which this change in cultivation fed is something that we all know about. To deal with it, the US is bringing massive pressure on Latin American governments.

Duncan Campbell (*Guardian*, 3 June 1998) reports that Bolivia, Peru and Colombia are under orders to destroy all their coca crops not used for 'traditional ' purposes, that is, in medicines and drinks. The programme to put this into effect is leading to the dispossession of the peasants who have scratched a living by growing the plant since the tin industry collapsed in the mid-'80s. The peasants see it as a strategy of dispossession to enable foreign mineral companies to move in. Poverty, meanwhile, which follows from such programmes, increases pressures on immigration. Only seven years after the fall of the Berlin Wall, the United States has had to erect another wall, just as morally loathsome: a wall which separates the United States from Mexico, impoverished by debt and unjust terms of trade, whose citizens cannot be kept out any other way. The Berlin Wall was widely seen as the symbol of a corrupt, unjust and failed regime. How long before this other wall, and the economic and moral order it symbolizes, also comes down?

CHAPTER 5

KINGDOMS WITHOUT JUSTICE

> The twentieth century has been characterized by three developments of great political importance: the growth of democracy, the growth of corporate power and the growth of corporate propaganda as a means of protecting corporate power against democracy.
>
> Andrew Carey, *Taking the Risk out of Democracy*, 1995

With an eye on the barbarian tribes overrunning the Roman empire, St Augustine asked some fundamental questions about the rule of law. 'Remove justice, and what are kingdoms but gangs of criminals on a large scale? What are criminal gangs but petty kingdoms?' (*City of God*, AD 413–26.) Fifteen hundred years later in *Hidden Agendas*, John Pilger poses similar questions about the operations of the world's great trading companies. They are, he says, totalitarian by nature, not the equivalent of independent sovereign states but the shock troops of the imperial powers, and their clubs like the OECD and the WTO 'exist to "open up" countries to "competitiveness", a current euphemism for plunder'. In 1992 John Gray was prepared to argue that corporations exist within, and are subject to the constraints of, a global competitive economy, and this keeps them properly in check (*Moral Foundations*). Even in 1998 Gray believed that the multinationals are 'as exposed to the vagaries of late modern societies as governments', and that they operate in a fog of uncertainty (*False Dawn*). States are not marginal players and can help rein in the power of these giant organizations. Who is right? Are modern transnationals the equivalent of St Augustine's robber bands, or are they virtuous subjects of the commonwealth, doing everything they can to promote the common good?

As the struggle against Nazism, one of the darkest barbarisms in human history, entered its final phases, Karl Polanyi set a dilemma before his contemporaries. Contrary to most popular rhetoric Polanyi insisted that it was market liberalism and not Communism that was truly utopian. It envisages a world where power and compulsion are absent. The market view of society equates economics with contractual relationships and contractual relationships with freedom:

> The radical illusion was fostered that there is nothing in human society that is not derived from the volition of individuals and that could not, therefore, be removed again by their volition. Vision was limited by the market which 'fragmented' life into the producer's sector that ended when his product reached the market, and the sector of the consumer for which all goods sprang from the market. The one derived his income 'freely' from the market, the other spent it 'freely' there. Society as a whole remained invisible. The power of the State was of no account, since the less its power, the smoother the market mechanism would function. Neither voters, nor owners, neither producers, nor consumers could be held responsible for such brutal restrictions of freedom as were involved in the occurrence of unemployment and destitution.
>
> (*The Great Transformation*, 1944)

This world was built on bad faith. We have to acknowledge the role of power in society frankly, and not pretend that it is 'nowhere'. We have to accept the need for planning, Polanyi argued, but at the same time take stringent steps to preserve individual freedoms. The rediscovery of society could be the end of freedom, as in Fascism, a return to the Dark Ages, or it could be its rebirth.

Polanyi did not envisage the ideology of market liberalism surviving the end of the Second World War. There he was spectacularly wrong, for not only did it survive, but it has become hegemonic. Two developments in particular have characterized its growth in the past twenty years: the burgeoning power of transnational corporations and the hyper-reality of speculative finance – the twin realities of 'globalization'. These developments, the face of economic growth today, pose serious threats both to sustainability and to democracy. The individualism Polanyi criticized has been immeasurably furthered by the information revolution which has enabled the 'money managers' to escape 'from community into the gap between communities where individualism has a free reign' (Daly and Cobb, *For the Common Good*, 1990). The power of people like the financier George Soros to destabilize national currencies has been amply demonstrated. Such power is the epitome of destructive individualism. Ironically Soros, who continues his speculative enterprises, now also believes that the project of 'extending the market mechanism to all domains has the potential of destroying society' (*New Statesman*, 31 October 1997).

Globalization has meant a *de facto* loss of power and control for the nation state. Many of us might be tempted to cheer: after all, the nation state has lain at the root of many of the bloodiest conflicts in history. But this development has profound implications for economic democracy. Adam Smith assumed, as did Keynes at Bretton Woods, that the nation state would be the primary player in the economic marketplace. In words which are now often cited, Keynes recommended that economic entanglement between nations should be minimized rather than maximized: 'Ideas, knowledge, art, hospitality, travel – these are things which should of their nature be international. But let goods be homespun whenever it is reasonably and conveniently possible; and above all let finance be primarily national.' (Cited in Daly, *Beyond Growth*, 1996.) When finance is national then, in a democratic state, it is subject to some measure of democratic control. When it is international, who controls it?

Big Brother Once Again

The collapse of Stalinism in 1989 ushered in 'the end of history', the triumph of the free-market version of democracy. We finally got rid of Big Brother. Or did we? The rhetoric of bodies like the World Trade Organization is that of 'free' trade, but, in fact, trade is largely controlled by a small number of huge corporations. The largest 10 transnational companies (TNCs) control assets which represent three times the total income of the world's poorest 38 countries, with a population of over one billion people. Of the world's 100 largest economies, 50 are TNCs. The leading 350 TNCs, employing only the tiniest fraction of the world's population, control 40 per cent of global trade. *The Economist* found a five-firm concentration for 12 global industries. In consumer durables, 5 firms control 70 per cent of the world market; in car, airline, aerospace, electrical and steel industries 5 firms control 50 per cent; in oil, computer and media industries they control 40 per cent. And the mega-mergers go on all the time. 'Big business just got bigger,' announced the *Guardian* on 14 October 1997, reporting a spate of mergers which accounted for 10 per cent of British Gross Domestic Product. The result of big mergers, the article pointed out, is less choice for consumers and more opportunity for the suppliers to raise prices. Globalization, in other words, does not increase competition but shrinks it. And the mergers go on, and are set to continue. 'The day of the small or medium-sized car firm is over,' said the head of Volvo, who resigned when a proposed merger with Renault failed. Only the largest companies can survive in the global market-place.

In Keynes's vision, at the end of the Second World War, international trade was to be harmonious trading between equals. He had in mind the nineteenth-century economist Ricardo's theory of comparative advantage as the theoretical underpinning (though British imperialism had never paid more than lip-service to this). According to this theory, if Britain exports coal to Portugal and Portugal exports wine to Britain, both countries gain. Today, however, comparative advantage has no place: 40 per cent of world trade is now trade *within* companies. The growth of ever-larger corporations is driven by the quest for profit, not only because of the control of the market they make possible but because they enable 'downsizing' – a euphemism for making people redundant. From 1980 to 1993 the Fortune 500 industrial firms shed nearly 4.4 million jobs, increased their sales by 1.4 per cent and assets by 2.3 per cent. Remuneration of senior executives increased by 6.1 times to $3.8 million (Korten, *When Corporations Rule the World*, 1995). In Britain privatization of the utilities led to similar results with top executives awarding themselves huge rises.

Profits for the company are made by seeking low-wage manufacturing sites from which to export to high-wage consumer markets. So called 'free-trade zones', of which there are now more than 80 operating in 30 countries, and 'export-processing zones', of which there are more than 120, offer transnationals cheap non-union labour kept in check by harsh anti-strike legislation, a range of subsidies and unrestricted repatriation of profits. In these zones conditions equal or surpass the worst excesses of the early days of the Industrial Revolution. Thus a report on a knitwear factory in an export zone in Sri Lanka found workers constantly exposed to liquid chemicals and fumes: 'Conditions are appalling. A working week can be over 110 hours. After about 4 years, an employee's health will have deteriorated to such a degree that they are unfit to continue working.' (Rowell, *Green Backlash*, 1996.) John Pilger found that in Saigon women work for the equivalent of £12 a month from 7 am to 9 pm: 'They must never stop . . . They are given a hygiene card which allows them to do their personal hygiene only three times a day, each time taking no more than five minutes.' (*Hidden Agendas*, 1998.) In the face of major disasters, such as the leak at the Union Carbide plant in Bhopal in 1986, the host country finds it has very little legal power over the transnational company. Up to 16,000 people died as a result of the Bhopal accident and people are still dying. Union Carbide was sued for $10 billion, but settled for $470 million and left the country. No one was prosecuted.

Even countries like Britain now have to play this game. The Department of Trade and Industry seeks to attract foreign investment by claiming: 'The UK has the least onerous labour regulations in Europe, with few restrictions on working hours, overtime and holidays. . . . There is no legal requirement to recognize a trade union. Many industries operate shift work, and 24-hour, seven-days-a-week production for both men and women.' The use of free-trade zones and the utilization of cheap labour shows that the transnationals owe no allegiance to any community. They take advantage of high incomes in the North while failing significantly to raise the standard of living in the South. Singer and Ansari point out that the claim that they contribute to development is flawed because their overall objective is maximization of profit. Instead of encouraging income equality they employ a small, elite, semi-skilled and highly skilled labour force whose incomes are substantially higher than the incomes of other workers (*Rich and Poor Countries*, 1988). Neither are they interested primarily in products which benefit poorer countries, but rather in goods for which there is already a lucrative world market and which are available only to the wealthy minority in developing countries. The Birmingham Trades Union group comments, 'By introducing the ideology of Western consumer society TNCs have neglected the pressing basic needs of the mass of underprivileged persons of the developing countries.' (*Jobs Crisis and the Multinationals*, no date.)

The technology of transnational industries could theoretically spill over into local industries but in general this has not happened. Research and development is primarily made with a view to the requirements of the developed countries. Much of the new technology has nothing to contribute to Southern countries and may, as in the development of synthetics, be positively harmful. Transnational investment can lead to the squeezing out of local firms and consequent increase in the concentration of economic power whose priorities are not dictated by the overall good of any country's population but rather by the amount of profit they can make. Investment by transnationals often diverts finance and energy away from the rural areas where most people live. Where it does not, however, as in the 'agribusiness' of the 'Green Revolution', the effects can be disastrous. The introduction of soya bean cultivation in Brazil, for example, has downgraded the quality of the local diet by occupying food-producing land and causing prices to rise. The introduction of cash crops throughout sub-Saharan Africa has taken the most fertile land away from direct food production. In this way, say Gaffikin and Nickson, 'they not only exploit the food crisis, but are significantly responsible for it in the first place' (*Jobs Crisis and the Multinationals*). The high technology export-crop model of agribusiness increases hunger because, 'Scarce land, credit, water and technology are pre-empted for the export market. Most hungry people are not affected by the market at all. . . . The profits flow to corporations that have no interest in feeding hungry people without money.' (Barnet, *The Lean Years*, 1981.)

It is an irony that after decades of free-market propaganda against the iniquities of centralized planning, successful corporations now maintain more control over the economies defined by their product networks than the planners in Moscow ever achieved, as David Korten points out in *When Corporations Rule the World* (1995). One version of Big Brother has been replaced by another, the state by the omnipresent corporation, and there are disturbing similarities between the versions. Companies are not simply places where one goes to work: they expect employees to adopt particular lifestyles and values. The corporation is extending this authoritarian rule beyond the boundaries of the corporation itself over a far larger network of organizations in ways that allow the core to consolidate its control while reducing its responsibility for the well-being of any member of the network.

The power of transnationals is shown by the OECD's proposal for a Multilateral Agreement on Investment (MAI), which they have had a large hand in drafting. Its aim is to liberalize conditions for these companies through the principles of non-discrimination, so that foreign investors must receive the same treatment as domestic companies. It seeks to do away with entry restrictions, so that governments cannot restrict foreign investment in any form, and to do away with conditionality. Under the agreement, the World Development Movement points out, citizens will lose long-standing democratic rights while transnationals will be given new powers, including the powers to sue governments and local authorities for non-compliance ('A Dangerous Leap in the Dark', 1997). As they argue, this means that the rights of companies are elevated over those of countries and their citizens. Bermuda, for example, has resisted McDonald's attempts to set up shop. Under the new regulations, a corporation with far greater wealth than Bermuda can muster would be able to compel it to give in. It is thus a charter for the neo-colonialism of the TNCs and their global throw-away culture. Significantly, the US negotiator concerned with this agreement has seen to it that states and local authorities in the US have agreed opt-out clauses, a choice not offered to the developing world.

The aim of the agreement, the World Development Movement point out, is to liberalize investment in developing countries. Smaller countries are being told that they must join or they will not get invest-ment. The MAI would prohibit countries from imposing conditions that would protect citizens' health, workers' rights, minorities, local communities or the environment. Multinationals could claim com-pensation for 'expropriation' of their right to pollute the environment and damage citizens' health. Local authorities would not be able to implement policies to control inappropriate foreign investment, or utilize policies to ensure that investors employ local people. This is already happening through the Bretton Woods institutions, a global bureaucracy which usurps decisions properly the preserve of elected bodies. As Deepak Nayar, former chief economic adviser to the Indian government, put it, the TNCs are emerging as a new global govern-ment, a World Inc. Ltd, with the G7 (or G7 + 1 as we must now say) as the board of directors (cited in Cavanagh, et al., *Beyond Bretton Woods*, 1994). Under the new proposals international finance rather than democratic governments will be in the driving seat.

A similar thing is happening through the agricultural agreement of the Uruguay Round mentioned in the last chapter. In effect, sover-eignty over national food policy is transferred from national governments to an unaccountable trade body in Geneva. Again, this poses an acute threat to democracy and accountability. US corporations have played a key role, supported by the Department of Agriculture, which sees diminishing productivity in the Philippines, Thailand and China as a potential for US exports. No regard is paid to the real needs of the countries concerned, but only to commercial self-interest.

The question of intellectual property rights, the sticking point for the biodiversity agreement in Rio, also hits Third World countries (the South) by raising the cost of technology transfer. Under the new rules, World Trade Organization members have to provide for the protection of plant varieties, for example, either through patents or through a system of royalty collection. The result, according to Oxfam, will be that companies will be able to pursue patented seeds with the full force of international law. Consequently farmers could be penal-ized for saving seeds for planting in future seasons or for exchange with other farmers.

For all these reasons Daly argues that international free trade is intrinsically harmful: 'It sins against allocative efficiency by making it difficult for nations to internalize external costs; it sins against distributive justice by widening the disparity between labour and capital in high-wage countries; it sins against community by demanding more mobility and by further separating ownership and control; and it sins against macroeconomic stability.' It also leads to a situation where each country is trying to live beyond its own absorptive and regenerative capacities by exporting waste and is therefore ecologically unsustainable (*Beyond Growth*, 1996).

When Polanyi was writing in 1944 it seemed that a measure of real democracy was at last within people's grasp. It proved elusive. If the threat from the omnicompetent state is slowly fading, the threat from the omnicompetent corporation has yet to be tackled.

Finance and Hyper-reality

The theoretician of consumer capitalism, Jean Baudrillard, talks of 'hyper-reality'. Often his formulations seem extravagant, but they make perfect sense against the background of the present financial markets.

The $1 billion that George Soros made by speculating on the British pound (causing the pound to fall 41 per cent against the yen over eleven months up to September 1992), and the collapse of Barings bank in 1995 (due to betting on futures by a minor player in Singapore) have brought the new realities of the financial world to everyone's attention. In fact, it could be argued that this development simply spells out the logic of financial activity, as Aristotle realized nearly two and a half thousand years ago.

Money is in origin a token, a means to aid exchange. A coin is a measure of what is deemed to be equivalent value: if you are willing to exchange one cow for three amphorae of olive oil, I can generalize the value by saying both are worth ten drachmae. In order to prevent cheating, however, money itself is given a value – coined out of precious metals. The move to paper money in the eighteenth century at first remained tied to precious metals through the promise on the note to redeem it for one pound's or one dollar's-worth of gold. The illusion that this fostered was abandoned finally when the United States came off the gold standard in 1971. Money was now, as it had been effectively for some time, a token of exchange with no intrinsic value.

The next step came with computerization and the linking of the world's stockmarkets. Investments in stocks and shares has, of course, always been a gamble, morally justified by the goods and employment it made possible. Now, however, casino capitalism has been born. Traders on the world stockmarket now bet on the rise and fall of prices and the likely future price of commodities. As Robert Reich put it in *The Next American Frontier* (1983), 'The set of symbols developed to represent real assets has lost the link with any actual productive activity. Finance has progressively evolved into a sector all its own, only loosely connected to industry.' These forms of specula-tion only came into being in the 1970s. Now they are the world's biggest money-spinners. About a trillion dollars a day is transferred on international markets. Only 18 per cent of this supports investment or trade, according to the Federal Reserve Board of New York, the rest is pure speculation, buying low and selling high.

The absurd nature of this situation, at once both farcical and corrupt, is spelt out by David Korten in *When Corporations Rule the World*. In the crash of the New York stockmarket in 1987 investors lost one trillion dollars in two months, corresponding to an eighth of all human products in the United States. This amount of money would feed the entire world for two years. But, he writes:

> In fact this $1 trillion could not have fed the world for even five minutes for the simple reason that people can't eat money. They eat food, and the collapse of the stock-market values did not in itself increase or decrease the world's actual supply of food by so much as a single grain of rice. Only the prices at which shares in particular companies could be bought and sold changed. There was no change in the productive capacity of any of those.

This is clearly what lies behind Baudrillard's views of 'hyper-reality'. In this fantasy world 'growth' means an increase in the amount of money circulating in the financial economy, independent of any increase in the output of real goods and services. Even the right-wing US President (1989–93) George Bush realized that in any other sphere this 'growth' would be called inflation. What the process amounts to, Korten correctly points out, is an extractive tax on those who are truly productive. The rewards of the financial traders go through the roof, while those of nurses, textile workers or teachers through the floor. 'The extractive investor is taking advantage of price fluctuations to claim a portion of the value created by productive investors and by people doing real work.'

Another form of extractive activity is the buying, re-packaging and re-selling of amenities in the interest of international finance. At the beginning of 1998 we learned that the finance manager of the Japanese firm Nomura earned £40 million in a year by buying up pubs, homes and betting shops, and re-selling them. His biggest success was British Rail's rolling-stock – paid for by the taxpayer for the previous fifty years – sold cheaply to Nomura in the mid-1990s, and re-sold at a profit of £390 million.

In the course of all this activity a great deal of money is 'made' but nothing productive is added to society's stock. The extra profit is not there to be invested in public utilities but to make obscene profits for those individuals and companies at the heart of international finance. As Marxist rhetoric for decades described them, those involved in this activity are parasites, living off the value created by those not rewarded fairly for their work.

'Well,' we could say, 'so what? Good luck to them. Is it really doing any damage?' The answer is that, like the growth of huge firms, these developments also pose a threat to democracy, and in two ways. First, extreme inequality has historically always proved unsustainable and a threat to peace and order. On these grounds Daly in *Beyond Growth* argues not for a minimum but for a maximum wage. He suggests a ratio of one to ten between the lowest and the highest paid, which would 'serve the need for legitimate differences in rewards and incentives while respecting the fact that we are persons in community, not isolated atomistic individuals'. If pushed he would go to one to twenty, but at some point, he argues, distribution must become an issue. In 1960 average pay after tax for chief executives was about twelve times that of the average for factory workers. By 1974 this ratio had risen to thirty-five. In 1995 *Business Week* put it at 135 to 1. Daly comments: 'Bonds of community break at or before a factor of one hundred. Class warfare is already beginning.' Lisa Buckingham (*Guardian*, 17 April 1998) notes that senior executives, whose pay rises are way above the rate of inflation, argue that they need the incentive of huge bonuses while at the same time employees must be motivated by fear of losing their jobs. In this arena, she comments, 'justice is way out on a limb'. We could ask whether the performance of top managers has increased by a factor of twelve in the intervening twenty years: this could easily be measured, and, since the period covers recessionary years, the evidence is unlikely to be favourable. But there are other considerations. As we have seen, greed (*pleonexia*) for Aristotle is at the heart of injustice. Perhaps he had in mind what he learned from his teacher, Plato, about injustice as a disorder of the soul. Unjust, greedy people suffer from disordered psyches says the philosopher Judith Shklar, taking up Plato's ideas: 'Irrationality, insolence, uncontrollable desires, aggressiveness, and sheer stupidity are all, in their way, psychic diseases that make us unjust, and we do such people no favour at all if we allow them to continue to live in such a state.' (*The Faces of Injustice*, 1990.) Of course the fat-cat salaries are an absurdity, utterly undeserved, which is why their recipients need to talk themselves up the whole time. But in seeking to ground them, it is not envy which motivates us, but simple concern for their disordered souls. . . .

But aside from the dangers posed by an unjust order, there is also a more direct threat to democracy, recognized by the business world itself. Thus *Business Week* comments, 'In this new market . . . billions can flow in or out of an economy in seconds. So powerful has this force of money become that some observers now see the hot-money set becoming a sort of shadow world government – one that is irretrievably eroding the concept of the sovereign powers of the nation state.' (Quoted in Korten, *When Corporations Rule the World*, 1995.) The former Chairman of Citicorp, Walter Wriston, agrees, noting that the new financial system 'does not sit too well with many sovereign governments because they correctly perceive [it] as an attack on the very nature of sovereign power' (Cavanagh, et al., *Beyond Bretton Woods*, 1994).

As an illustration, consider the way these forms of speculation damage communities. They were responsible, for example, for the Mexican crash of 1994 which required a US bail-out, which in turn required austerity measures which put 750,000 people out of work. The interest rates of 90 per cent that this led to made many Mexicans bankrupt. Similarly Zambian interest rates went up to more than 100 per cent under the impact of an IMF structural adjustment programme. Foreign speculators doubled their money while the textile industry was starved of cash.

A further threat to democracy is posed by the power big money brings with it. The wealth of big business has been used, Andrew Rowell has shown, to finance anti-environmental groups and to promote the values of private property, free markets and limited government. 'Overtly and covertly,' says Rowell in *Green Backlash* (1996), 'by stealth and by design, big business has perverted the democratic process by buying politicians, by bribing them, by funding "independent" think-tanks, by forming "corporate front groups", by bullying citizens, by lobbying and by lying – all in the name of profit.' Corporations fund the Competitive Enterprise Institute, the Political Economy Research Institute and the Heritage Foundation among others, all dedicated to promoting a 'free' market deregulatory agenda. Widely publicized debates about political funding have emphasized that corporate money is now a fundamental force in both British and American politics. Because the shareholders for the great companies are in turn financial institutions, individual shareholders have effectively no say in the affairs of the company. Since financiers are engaged in 'a near continuous shuffle for profit', Rowell argues that even large shareholder accountability is largely illusory.

Under the Reagan and Bush administrations in the USA (1981–93) the corporate anti-regulation agenda was furthered by the repeal of nearly sixty major environmental, health, safety and other regulations, affecting car pollution, hazardous wastes and health standards for asbestos, chromium and cadmium. In Britain in the same period the pact between government and business was sealed by directorships and consultancies for former ministers and backbenchers. As Rowell says, 'By also representing corporations, MPs who are elected to represent constituents must suffer at least some conflict in interest ... what is normally good for a corporation is rarely directly beneficial to the public.'

The corporations fund large front groups like the Citizens for Sensible Control of Acid Rain in the United States which is set up to defeat acid rain legislation and funded by the electricity companies, or the Council for Energy Awareness, funded by the nuclear industry to promote its aims. One of the most prominent anti-environment groups, the Wise Use movement, formed in 1988, was able according to Rowell to prevent the ratification of the Rio Biodiversity Treaty in 1992. Amoco, BP, Chevron, Dow Chemical, Du Pont, Exxon, Shell, Texaco and Union Carbide are among those who fund the Global Climate Coalition, which 'have a vested interest in seeing any international treaties on CO_2 reduction weakened' (*Green Backlash*). As we have seen at Kyoto in 1997, and now at the G8 summit in 1998, they have been successful.

Environmental challenges are taken so seriously that a number of environmentalists or anti-nuclear protestors have been killed or critically injured in assassination attempts in recent years: Chico Mendes in Brazil, Ken Saro-Wiwa in Nigeria, Judi Bari and Stephanie McGuire in the United States, and Hilda Murrell and William McCrae in Britain.

Andrew Rowell recounts McGuire's case in *Green Backlash*. She was protesting against Proctor and Gamble's cellulose mill in Florida. In 1992 she was beaten, slashed with a razor, and raped by two assailants who were reported to have said: 'This is what you get for talking about P & G.' No one was ever prosecuted. Ken Saro-Wiwa was executed by the Nigerian government in November 1995 for protesting at environmental pollution caused by Shell. The company was able to pollute through the complicity of the unelected military government, who have profited handsomely from oil revenues at the expense of the Ogoni people.

Justice, we are told by contemporary market apologists, is not the epitome of the virtues at all, but simply something we need to rectify unbalanced situations. But what if the world economic system has become nothing less than an organized criminal conspiracy, in which law is flouted and the poor suffer? In *Hidden Agendas* Pilger cites the example of Haiti, where every industry except coffee is controlled by US multinationals: 'As a direct result of this "free market", half the children die before they reach the age of five and thousands of workers earn eightpence an hour making Walt Disney pyjamas for Western children. Life expectancy is fifty-three years.' The world that Pilger documents is one of large-scale robber bands, of 'kingdoms without justice', in which the life of the poor is simply expendable. It is not only ecologically unsustainable, as we saw in the last chapter, but morally unsustainable as well. It is not too much to say that the possibility of a human future is contingent on the re-establishment of justice in what is now a global kingdom. Another transformation, greater than that brought by the Industrial Revolution, is imperative.

CHAPTER 6

SEEKING JUSTICE

Cease to do evil,
learn to do good:
seek justice,
rescue the oppressed

Isaiah of Jerusalem, eighth century BC

Sustainable development will require a change of heart, a renewal of the mind, and a healthy dose of repentance. These are all religious terms, and that is no coincidence, because a change in the fundamental principles we live by is a change so deep that it is essentially religious whether we call it that or not.

Herman Daly, *Beyond Growth*, 1996

The process which led both to the advantages which the well-off in today's world enjoy, and to the poverty and suffering of the many was the product of a Great Transformation. In view of the injustice which that system has produced and continues to produce, and in view of the threat to the planet which is part and parcel of the same process, it is clear that another transformation, equally as great, is imperative. Humanity is on a collision course with natural boundaries, warns the 1997 Club of Rome report, *Factor Four*: 'If we fail to change course soon enough and the collision occurs, nature will survive the event *somehow*. Humanity will not.'

We have to make a decision. Is it really the case that the damage caused by the current economic model has already gone so far that only global action can stave off disaster, or is talk of 'crisis' just scaremongering by a lunatic fringe of Green activists? Which side represents common sense – *The Economist*, Wilfred Beckerman, but also the Oxfam economists urgently seeking economic growth to improve the lot of the world's poor, or Herman Daly and the Worldwatch Institute, urgently advocating a transition to a steady-state economy?

Polanyi argued that the real choice between market utopianism and the combination of planning with freedom that he called socialism was moral and religious. Over the past two decades, an increasing number of political thinkers and ecologists, and, what is more surprising, economists, have come to the same view. Perhaps the most striking account has been offered by Rudolf Bahro, the radical Marxist turned Green activist who died of leukaemia in the winter of 1997. Bahro became aware that conventional Marxist accounts did not touch the heart of the social and economic problem, and that Green politics too remained within the bounds of market discourse. The problem, he said, went far beyond the competing claims of political programmes to the basic psychological structure of Western humanity. It is this that is taking us to disaster. He agreed with E.P. Thompson that Western society was characterized by 'exterminism', a logic of annihilation which was expressed in the compulsion of growth and the market society. For him the most important political discipline is seeking the truth about ourselves. What we need to avoid catastrophe is an anthropological revolution, a jump in the evolution of the human spirit. Following the Swiss philosopher Jean Gebser, he traces human consciousness through the archaic, magic, and mythic periods to the mental, characterized by the determination to transcend nature. This is the mode of consciousness which drove the great era of scientific discovery and the Industrial Revolution. It has accomplished amazing things but, at the end of this period, the frustrations which resulted from its denials of the body, nature and the feminine led to the concentration camps and two world wars. Gebser spoke of a fifth, or integral, structure of consciousness, and it is this which Bahro believed is now emerging, the heart of the coming transformation. Whether or not we are able to move from the logic of annihilation to the logic of salvation depends on how quickly a critical mass of the population can achieve this integral structure of consciousness. As he argued in *Avoiding Social and Ecological Catastrophe* (1994), 'No order can save us which simply limits the excesses of our greed. Only spiritual mastery of the greed itself can help us.' In his view the ecological crisis is the last, but also the greatest, opportunity for achieving a new human articulation.

Irrespective of the details of Bahro's argument – a fascinating critical tour of the world's religious traditions by someone who always remained an atheist – I find his central points absolutely right: we do face a crisis, and this is a fundamentally 'spiritual' problem, using that word in its broadest sense. In our present situation the spiritual is the economic, and vice versa. The new spirituality recognizes the imperative, as Kothari puts it (Cavanagh, et al., *Beyond Bretton Woods*, 1994), to 'transcend reductionist economics and the technocratic managerial ethic and self-consciously and politically align ourselves with those peoples, ecosystems and nations that have been rendered impoverished and destitute by the current patterns of economic development and ecological imperialism.' How, then, is that practically possible?

The Limits and Possibilities of a Technical Fix

Everybody likes to have their cake and eat it. Could we perhaps continue with the same level of consumption we currently enjoy in the North and rely on technology to sort out our problems? The short answer to this is 'no', but on the other hand there is no reason to doubt that many important changes and improvements can be made at the technical level, and in terms of changes to current practice. These, though not the 'answer' to the environmental crisis, remain imperative. The Club of Rome (1997) report sets out ways in which resource use can be halved and productivity doubled at the same time. The authors instance the 'hypercar' which will save 80–95 per cent of present fuel use. Both Peugeot and General Motors hope to have electrically powered cars in production by 2004 (*The Times*, 31 January 1998). The Club of Rome authors give many examples of houses and offices which are being designed to minimize energy use. The Worldwatch group calculated that if the 300 million incandescent bulbs in use in India were replaced with compact fluorescents it would avoid the need for building 8000 megawatts of generating capacity (Starke, ed., *State of the World 1992*). The efficiency of refrigerators has already more than doubled. In order to reduce carbon emissions, solar and geothermal energy will have to replace non-renewable energy. Solar or wind electricity can be used to produce hydrogen via the electrolysis of water. Worldwatch comment in the same 1992 survey that, 'The solar/hydrogen combination could become the cornerstone of a new global energy economy based on renewable resources.' In their view no completely new technologies are needed to switch to a solar-based economy. Douthwaite (*Short Circuit*, 1996) gives many examples of current small-scale initiatives using solar, wind or biomass energy. Extrapolating from these he suggests that the electricity production and supply of the future will use the national grid not only as a source of supply but as a battery. 'Many households will produce their own electricity ... whenever they have more than they need they will "bank" the surplus by feeding it into the grid; whenever they need more power ... they will take the required surplus from the mains ... the grid will become a common carrier for electricity rather than the distribution arm of a monopoly supplier.' Southern countries will be able to switch from AC to DC supply, using renewable batteries.

All sorts of devices are available for more efficient use of water: new flush toilets use a fraction of the water of conventional WCs; new showers use four to five times less water; efficient use of rainwater can reduce public supply withdrawals by 90 per cent.

Recycling is a fundamental part of the new technology. Most materials today are discarded after one use. It is true that entropy means that something is always lost in the recycling process, but it nevertheless usually saves energy and reduces pollution. In a sustainable economy, Worldwatch argue, most materials for industry will be recycled goods (*State of the World 1992*). Much can be done to cut down waste. We all know the extent of waste involved in food packaging. This needs to be reduced by tax or government regulations. If we moved from cans to reusable bottles for our drinks, for example, as Denmark has done, energy use per container can be reduced by 90 per cent. Water-soluble plastics, which can be recycled, can be used for food and other packaging.

The Club of Rome authors (*Factor Four*, 1997) are fundamentally hopeful, but they nevertheless conclude:

> Productive use of the gifts we borrow from the earth and from each other can gain us more time to search. But like any tool, it can only help us a little towards, and can never substitute for, the renewal of our polity, our ethical principles and our spirituality. The resources that we need most urgently to rediscover and to use more fully and wisely are not in the physical world, but remain hidden within each one of us.

Economics as if People Mattered

I have argued throughout that there is a fundamental contrast between a profit-driven and a needs-driven vision of the 'economy'. How do we move from one to the other? The *United Nations Development Report 1997* remarks that, 'In many respects the world is sailing through the current era of globalization with neither compass nor map.' In fact, map and compass are available: the question is rather whether we care to use them. As an example of such instruments we could take the six principles that David Korten has outlined in *When Corporations Rule the World* (1995), which helpfully sketch out the architecture of the transformation we need. In summary they are these:

- The principle of environmental sustainability, according to which rates of use of renewable resources do not exceed the rates at which the ecosystem is able to regenerate them.
- The principle of economic justice – which means that a sustainable economy will have to see that everyone's needs are met.
- The principle of biological and cultural diversity, which speaks for itself.
- The principle of people's sovereignty, which involves re-locating power in civil society.
- The principle of intrinsic responsibility, by which we internalize costs, and do not externalize them.
- The principle of common heritage, according to which we recognize that the environmental resources of the planet and accumulated knowledge of the species are common heritage resources.

Such principles could provide a very adequate map and compass for the coming transformation. Fundamental to the implementation of such principles is Herman Daly's 'steady-state' economy. It has to be emphasized that this is not a 'no-growth' economy. On the contrary, understanding economy in its proper sense, the sustaining of life, there is infinite room for growth in all those things which make life worth living. However, given the constraints of growing population and fixed environmental limits, whether of resources or, more importantly of sinks (oceans and forests), it is, as Daly describes it in *Steady-State Economics* (1992), 'an economy with constant stocks of people and artefacts, maintained at some desired, sufficient levels by low rates of maintenance "throughput"'. For this to function, 'institutions' would be needed to stabilize population (he favours transferable birth licences), for stabilizing the stock of physical artefacts and keeping 'throughput' (population multiplied by resource use) below ecological levels, and for limiting the degree of inequality. With regard to the second, he believes that limits must be imposed on resource extraction and that then prices will allocate or ration the fixed aggregate among firms. 'For non-renewables with renewable substitutes, the quotas should be set so that the resulting price of the non-renewable resource is at least as high as the price of the nearest renewable substitute. For non-renewables with no close renewable substitute, the quota would reflect a purely ethical judgement concerning the relative importance of present versus future wants.' With regard to the third, he argues that redistribution is the only cure for poverty, and that we cannot expect growth to do the job.

Given Daly's warnings about the limits of 'throughput' fundamental changes are essential in both. Stabilizing world population remains a top priority. At present 5.77 billion, and growing at 80 million a year, Worldwatch (*State of the World 1992*) estimate 8 billion as the maximum for the planet's carrying capacity, allowing a decent quality of life to all. To stabilize at this number, they rightly point out, will take nothing less than a revolution in social values dependent on fundamental reforms in education, health care and the status of women, along with a massive global reordering of priorities. Daly's proposed 'birth tokens' are unlikely to find favour in the near future, but may be an idea forced on world governments in years to come. It is a question of setting individual autonomy against global survival.

Extensive changes in agricultural practice are called for, taking steps to reduce soil erosion, and reduce the use of pesticides and fertilizers. In 1992 the Rio Non-Governmental Organizations (NGOs) called for an agriculture which is 'ecologically sound, economically viable, socially just, culturally appropriate and based on a holistic scientific approach'. Such an agriculture would use locally available renewable resources, appropriate and affordable technologies and minimize the use of external and purchased inputs. Land Institute research in the United States has shown that, contrary to received wisdom, perennials can be high yielders. 'Using nature as model and mentor,' says the Club of Rome report (*Factor Four*, 1997), 'not as a nuisance to be evaded, yields the rich dividends of respecting several thousand million years of design experience in which everything that didn't work reliably was recalled by the manufacturer.' Unsustainable logging will have to be abandoned, at present at its worst in Asia and parts of South America, and more trees planted – Worldwatch calculated in 1992 that 130 million hectares (320 million acres) would be needed to meet fuel-wood needs and stabilize soil and resources in developing countries in the next ten years. Urgent action is also needed to conserve fish stocks.

Also essential will be an end to the absurdly wasteful situation whereby British consumers are encouraged to eat potatoes flown in from Egypt (when the bottom is already out of the British market because of overproduction), and where a pot of strawberry yoghurt carries with it 3494 km (2171 miles) of haulage! The present model of the economy is based on long-distance haulage for most products. All products carry what Schmidt-Bleek (cited in *Factor Four*, 1997) calls an 'ecological rucksack' – the amount of energy consumed in producing them. Thus the rucksack of a litre (2 pints) of orange juice is 100 kg (220 lb); that of a newspaper, 10kg (22 lb). This rucksack has to be reduced. The alternative model should be based on the relative self-sufficiency of communities, regions and nations as Keynes envisaged it. As a simple example, the Club of Rome report suggests the substitution of blackcurrant for orange juice in Northern Europe.

Given that taxation is going to be needed whatever the form of government, a radical re-orientation towards the taxing of polluting activities will be needed and an end to subsidies for high-consumption activity. At present coal and oil are not priced to reflect the damage their production and combustion cause. The Club of Rome report suggests an ecological tax reform which would increase energy prices by about 5 per cent annually, while cutting income tax. This will drive both domestic economy and technological innovation. One result might be, as Durning suggests in *How Much is Enough?* (1992), that local food would fall in price relative to pre-packed goods shipped from a distance, for instance, and there would be an inbuilt check in the waste involved in transportation.

As a way of de-coupling from the interest-driven market, greater local self-reliance can be fostered by establishing local currency and banking systems. These are not pipe dreams, but are already functioning in many areas of Europe and North America, as Douthwaite has illustrated in *Short Circuit* (1996). In the United States, almost a third of the population are members of credit unions.

Regulating the Global Economy

Acknowledging that there is no world government capable of regulating global capital, Daly goes on to say (*Beyond Growth*, 1996) that both the desirability and the possibility of such a world government is highly doubtful. On the other hand, the proposals of the *United Nations Human Development Report 1992* effectively amounted to extending the mandate of the UN to the economy, noting that, 'The present international economic order is undemocratic, against the interests of the majority of the world population, and thus extremely dangerous.' With the advent of the MAI we see that point reinforced. In their 1997 report, the UN comment: 'The UN has $4.6 billion a year to spend on economic and social development – less than the budget of New York's State University. This is the equivalent of 80 cent per human being, compared with the $134 a person spent annually on arms and the military. Is the United Nations too expensive for a globalizing world?' The final question highlights the fact that what is at stake is political will and the maintenance of present patterns of global hegemony. In Keynes's vision the Bretton Woods institutions were indeed to be part of the UN, and this is where they belong. The UN is the natural starting-point for bringing the global economy under democratic control, providing proper democracy can be established there. At present the IMF effectively functions like the UN Security Council, giving ultimate decisions to the biggest players. If genuine democracy were allowed, however, then the proposals of the UN report sound eminently common-sensical. Among them, in summary, are the following:

1 The replacement of the Bretton Woods institutions with a global central bank with the task of creating a common currency, maintaining price and exchange rate stability, and providing for a global adjustment of surpluses and deficits and for equal access to international loans. This would run alongside a system of global, regional, national and central banks which would be democratically accountable, and thus open to social and political priorities. Should this sound utopian we might recall that no less a person than George Soros is now advocating it. 'We will eventually have international regulation of markets,' he told the *New Statesman* (31 October 1997). 'What is lacking is the ability of society to impose some constraints on the market.'

2 The introduction of a system of progressive income tax to be collected automatically from the rich nations and to be distributed to the poor nations according to their income and development needs. Again, this approaches Keynes's vision of half a century ago.

3 The replacement of GATT (now WTO) by an international trade organization whose job it would be to ensure free and equal access to all forms of global trade. Given the problems we have seen with the implementation of GATT, and now the proposals for MAI, my own

view is that the emphasis should not be on 'free' trade, but on seeing that countries like, for example, the Windward Isles or Grenada, which have been reduced to dependence on a single crop by the accidents of colonial history, should not suffer as a consequence. Addressing the issue of primary commodities is crucial. The rise in interest in 'fair trade' as opposed to 'free trade' products shows that such a move could be popular.

4 The establishment of a new Development Security Council which could establish a broad policy framework for all global development issues, from food security to ecological security. As noted above, such a Council would have to be properly democratic, and not an extension of privilege to the powerful, like the present UN Security Council. A very small step was taken towards this with the establishment of the Global Environmental Facility at Rio 1992, though it is severely underfunded.

5 The establishment of an International Court of Economic Justice responsible for the management of the Global Commons: fish, water and forests. The urgent need for such an agency has been indicated year after year in recent times by disputes about fishing all over the world, and by unsustainable logging in Cambodia, Burma and Indonesia.

6 The establishment of international institutions and regulations to control transnational capital. The closure of tax havens, and thus the ending of capital flight would be part of this. The extreme volatility of the Asian markets at the end of 1997 ought to be sufficient to make the case for such a body.

In a rather pessimistic conclusion to a similar set of proposals Frances Stewart (in al-Haq, ed., *The UN and the Bretton Woods Institutions*, 1995) comments that their political feasibility does not seem high and that what countries can do for themselves is of greater relevance. The Bretton Woods institutions, however, were set up after the conflagration of the Second World War which had served to focus minds. What level of disorder does it take to focus minds once again on the urgent reform these institutions need?

Recovering Democracy

In the face of just such a question Robert Heilbroner wrote in *An Inquiry into the Human Prospect* (1975):

> Candour compels me to suggest that the passage through the gauntlet ahead may be possible only under governments capable of rallying obedience far more effectively than would be possible in a democratic setting. If the issue for mankind is survival, such governments may be unavoidable.

It is disturbing to say the least that Oxfam hold up as models of economic good practice countries that are among the most authoritarian on earth. Given the present arrangement of world power, the realization of Heilbroner's suggestion would certainly amount to a strategy for the survival of the wealthy and powerful. Far better, and ultimately the only sustainable way, is the recovery of democracy. As the Worldwatch team put it in 1992, 'The struggle for a livable world is about overcoming concentrations of economic power, about the universal human yearning for political freedoms, and about the fight for human rights and dignity.' But how realistic are the prospects for democracy?

In the West, as we have seen, the rhetoric of democracy and the rhetoric of free enterprise have been regarded as identical. It is especially incumbent on those of us who live in nations with long democratic traditions, which we certainly cannot value too highly, to recognize that we have hardly begun to find out what true democracy would look like. What we call democracies are in fact plutocracies, rule by the rich. 'One person, one vote' is not yet genuine democracy, though it is far better than what went before. In 1944 Polanyi wrote:

> Socialism is essentially the tendency inherent in an industrial civilization to transcend the self-regulating market by consciously subordinating it to a

democratic society. . . . From the point of view of the community as a whole, Socialism is merely the continuation of that endeavour to make society a distinctively human relationship of persons which in Western Europe was always associated with Christian tradition. From the point of view of the economic system it is, on the contrary, a radical departure from the immediate past in so far as it breaks with the attempt to make private money gains the general incentive to productive capacities and does not acknowledge the right of private individuals to dispose of the main instruments of production.

'Socialism' has become a 'boo' word, a sign that one is living in a distant past of factory chimneys and cloth caps, but all it amounts to, as Polanyi says, is democratic control of the self-regulating market. Friedman's insistence on the rigid separation of politics and economics is, of course, the shrewd recognition that to maintain wealth and power as they are, democracy won't do. Is there any chance of such control being established? More, perhaps, than one might think. In a study of what is currently happening to the nation state, the Professor of Politics at Leicester University, John Hofman, has suggested in his book *Beyond the State* (1995) that we are witnessing the decline of the centralized state which has caused so much conflict since the fifteenth century, and that this must be replaced, not by Balkanization and ethnic cleansing, but a network of regional, local and global bodies in which power is dispersed. That this would be consistent with extending the UN's remit to economics is obvious. The power to regulate commerce and trade and to tackle the problems of the environment would need to be taken up by every level of this power structure. Effectively what Hofman is proposing is some form of subsidiarity – the vesting of authority and responsibility in the smallest local unit. Economically this would make it possible to maintain a market system in which market power is balanced with political power at each level. As Korten points out (*When Corporations Rule the World*), local firms would enjoy a natural advantage and there would be less long-haul movement of people and goods. Korten advocates a market economy composed primarily of family enterprises, small scale co-ops, worker-owned firms, and neighbourhood and municipal corporations. Douthwaite agrees (*Short Circuit*, 1996). Firms that are owned and controlled by those working in them, he argues, regard work not only as a source of income but as one of the main ways in which people fulfil themselves. Unless we construct environments which foster such firms, in his view, 'Cut-throat international competition will ensure that in a few years time, highly paid jobs will only be available to the fortunate few.'

At exactly the same time as MacIntyre was concluding with his vision of new Benedictine communities, Rudolf Bahro, without any awareness of his work, was thinking along similar lines, inspired by the Italian Marxist Gramsci's idea of the Ordine Nuovo, the new order. Present-day society cannot regenerate itself, Bahro argued (*Avoiding Social and Ecological Catastrophe*, 1994), because it is too much part of the existing apparatus: 'Grass-roots communities of the Ordine Nuovo – in the form of a network of like-minded and like-feeling people everywhere, in nodal points of communitarian life – will be the first existential form of the new culture.' From a very different standpoint, Robert Bellah and a number of other leading sociologists in North America, advocate 'a new experiment in participatory democracy' in the American workplace and polity and a commitment to subsidiarity and decentralized power (*The Good Society*, 1991). Douthwaite meanwhile has traced and documented many such experiments. That his examples are primarily from the rich world is encouraging, for that is where the major problem lies. The basic transformation, said Bahro, will first of all be visualized by organized minorities, who for practical purposes will draft a new politics. Douthwaite shows it happening.

The Coming Transformation?

Douthwaite's small alternative communities show some of the cultural changes which are crucial to the coming transformation, for, over and above technical and political measures, it is here that the crunch comes. Beckerman argues that the world's great religions have, over millennia, failed to wean people off the craving to consume, and clearly believes the attempt is worthless. On the contrary, I reply, the present consumer culture is clearly feverish, a symptom of an illness, and we can recover from it with the realization that its promises are largely illusory and it simply cannot offer true human satisfaction. The cultural changes I look to in the coming transformation are fourfold.

First we must turn away from the corrosive individualism which the present economic order thrives on. We have already argued that humans are not 'by nature' rational utility maximizers, but, on the contrary, by nature co-operative. The well-advertised problems of crime and drugs in Western societies make it plain enough that the absence of community destroys us. The priority of individualism is part and parcel of the first Great Transformation. A return to community will be part and parcel of the second.

Secondly, no change is possible that leaves the consumer society as we know it in place. 'The North has to understand', write the Club of Rome authors (*Factor Four*, 1997), 'that sustainable development worldwide simply will not happen unless and until the North itself learns to live with far smaller per capita rates of resource consumption.' Consumerism is an addiction, like any drug, and we will have to be weaned off it. For this to happen, the advertising industry will certainly have to be regulated more tightly than it is. The ethic of conservation, and a real love for the earth, which has guided humankind for most of its history, and has been abandoned only in the past fifty years, has to be recovered. 'In the final analysis,' says Durning (*How Much is Enough?*), 'accepting and living by sufficiency rather than excess offers a return to what is, culturally speaking, the human home: to the ancient order of family, community, good work and good life; to a reverence for skill, creativity and creation.'

Thirdly there is the question which was put nearly two thousand years ago by the early Church Fathers about trades and professions which do not contribute to the common good. By their criteria, work in the arms trade or in the military would be illegitimate. Could these industries be re-directed? John Pilger (*Hidden Agendas*) cites someone who believes they could: Professor Michael Cooley, a leading aircraft design engineer. He insists that the 'defence' (i.e. arms) industry neither creates nor maintains jobs. Research spending in this area means that one job can cost as much as £600,000 to create. He goes on: 'I can list five thousand new products, beginning with systems for renewable energy to monitoring and control devices . . . that could combat our biggest killer, cardiovascular disease. . . . I'm not saying conversion is easy, but it can be done; it needs only the political will.'

Finally, the profit motive cannot be the central article of faith around which society is organized. So, for example, instead of seeking to monopolize knowledge for private gain (as does the current convention on intellectual property rights), we should encourage the sharing of knowledge and information recognizing with St Paul that we are all members one of another. It is the profit motive which is homogenizing global culture. Let us say 'No' to it, and 'No' to the ghastly thematization of life which sanitizes and dehistoricizes genuinely traditional establishments, and which is responsible for the relentless 'dumbing-down' of our culture over the past thirty years.

'The future of life on earth', says Durning in *How Much Is Enough?*, 'depends on whether we among the richest fifth of the world's people, having fully met our material needs, can turn to non-material sources of fulfilment.' 'Seek good and not evil, that you may live,' said the prophet Amos, some centuries before Aristotle gave his lectures on economics and ethics in Athens. 'Hate evil and love good, and establish justice.' And Isaiah was to say, a century or so later, 'Cease to do evil, learn to do good. Seek justice, rescue the oppressed.' For the prophets of Israel seeking justice was not just a moral imperative but an imperative for survival, and this is as true for us as it was for them. The changes needed are not impossible. Douthwaite (*Short Circuit*, 1996) shows through scores of examples that the techniques already exist which can lead to a better balance between the global and the local community, and that regional cultures can be reinvented and restored. It would be foolish and irresponsible to believe that this will happen overnight, or without a struggle. Too much wealth and power has been cornered for the few for that to be possible. On the other hand, despair is equally illegitimate. There are many signs that regeneration is possible, symbolized perhaps, as John Pilger hints, by the return of wildlife to Vietnam, two generations after its forests were drenched in Agent Orange. There are grounds for hope in the movement for fair trade, in the anti-consumerist movement, in Local

Exchange Trading Schemes (LETS) in which people trade skills without recourse to money, in environmental groups, in the new interest in organic farming, in the reaffirmation of indigenous cultures, in the continued growth of the women's movement, in the campaign against debt, and against the arms trade, and, not least, in the lively concern for a new spirituality. Through the changes Douthwaite, Daly and many others urge on us, justice can roll down in torrents, and mercy as a mountain stream, as one of the oldest voices in our cultural tradition, Isaiah of Jerusalem, put it. Nurtured by that hope, we can negotiate our way through the present Dark Ages if not to a final, then at least to a brighter, dawn.

BIBLIOGRAPHY

Aristotle, *Complete Works*, ed. J. Barnes, New Jersey, 1984

Augustine, St, *The City of God*, trans. H. Bettenson, Harmondsworth, 1984

Bahro, R., *Avoiding Social and Ecological Disaster: The Politics of World Transformation*, trans. from the German (published 1986) by D. Clarke, Bath, 1994

Barnet, R.J., *The Lean Years*, London, 1981

Baudrillard, J., *Symbolic Exchange and Death*, trans. from the French (published 1974) by I. Hamilton Grant, London, 1993

Beckerman, W., *In Defence of Economic Growth*, London, 1974

—, *Small is Stupid: Blowing the Whistle on the Greens*, London, 1995

Bellah, R. N., et al., *The Good Society*, New York, 1991

Bello, W., *Dark Victory: The United States, Structural Adjustment and Global Poverty*, London, 1994

Berry, W., *Home Economics*, San Francisco, 1987

Blumenfeld, Y., ed., *Scanning the Future*, London, 1999

Bradshaw, J., *Child Poverty and Deprivation in the UK*, London, 1990

Brown, L., C. Flavin and S. Postel, *Saving the Planet*, London, 1992

Buber, M., *I and Thou*, trans. from the German (published 1922) by W. Kaufmann, Edinburgh, 1970

Carey, A., *Taking the Risk out of Democracy: Propaganda in the US and Australia*, Sydney, 1995

Cavanagh, J., et al., *Beyond Bretton Woods: Alternatives to the Global Economic Order*, London, 1994

Centre for Economic Policy Research, 'European Economic Perspectives', March 1998

Chapra, U., *Towards a Just Monetary System*, Leicester, 1985

Club of Rome (E. von Weizsäcker, A. Lovins and H. Lovins), *Factor Four: Doubling Wealth, Halving Resource Use*, London, 1997

Cook, J., *Who Killed Hilda Murrell?*, London, 1985

Critchfield, R., *The Villagers*, New York, 1994

Daly, H., *Steady-State Economics*, London, 1992

—, *Beyond Growth*, Boston, 1996

Daly, H., and J. Cobb, *For the Common Good: Redirecting the Economy towards Community, the Environment and a Sustainable Future*, London, 1990

Douthwaite, R., *The Growth Illusion*, Totnes, 1992

—, *Short Circuit*, Totnes, 1996

Durkheim, E., *Suicide: A Study in Sociology*, New York, 1951

Durning, A.T., *How Much is Enough? The Consumer Society and the Future of the Earth*, London, 1992

Elliott, C., *Comfortable Compassion*, London, 1987

Engel, J.R., and J.G. Engel, eds, *Ethics of Environment and Development*, London, 1990

Engels, F., *The Conditions of the Working Class in England*, in Marx/Engels, *Collected Works*, vol. 4 (1845–46), Moscow, 1976

Friedman, M., and R. Friedman, *Free to Choose*, London, 1990

Gaffikin, F., and A. Nickson, *Jobs Crisis and the Multinationals*, Birmingham, n.d.

Gehlen, A., *Man in the Age of Technology*, New York, 1980

George, S., *A Fate Worse than Debt*, Harmondsworth, 1988

—, *The Debt Boomerang*, London, 1992

Gray, J., *The Moral Foundations of Market Institutions*, London, 1992

—, *False Dawn: The Delusions of Global Capitalism*, London, 1998

Haas, P., *Morality after Auschwitz*, Philadelphia, 1988

al-Haq, M., ed., *The UN and the Bretton Woods Institutions: New Challenges for the Twenty First Century*, London, 1995

Haug, W.F., *Critique of Commodity Aesthetics*, (first published Germany, 1967) Cambridge, 1986

Hayek, F. von, *Law, Legislation and Liberty*, vol. 2: *The Mirage of Social Justice*, London, 1976

Heelas, P., S. Lash and P. Morris, *Detraditionalization: Critical Reflections on Authority and Identity*, Oxford, 1996

Heilbroner, R., *An Inquiry into the Human Prospect*, New York, 1975

—, *The Nature and Logic of Capitalism*, New York, 1986

BIBLIOGRAPHY

Hofman, J., *Beyond the State*, Cambridge, 1995

Jameson, F., *Postmodernism, or, The Cultural Logic of Late Capitalism*, London, 1991

Körner, P., G. Maass, T. Siebold and R. Tetzlaff, *The IMF and the Debt Crisis*, London, 1986

Korten, D., *When Corporations Rule the World*, Connecticut, 1995

Lasch, C., *The Culture of Narcissism*, New York, 1991

Laslett, P., *The World We Have Lost*, London, 1965

Le Goff, J., *Medieval Civilization*, (first published France, 1964) Oxford, 1988

Lovelock, J., *Gaia: A New Look at Life on Earth*, Oxford, 1979

MacIntyre, A., *After Virtue*, (first published 1981) 2nd edn, London, 1985

Mandel, E., *Marxist Economic Theory*, London, 1968

Marx, K., 'Contribution to a Critique of Hegel's Philosophy of Law', *Collected Works*, vol. 3 (1844), Moscow, 1976

Mishan, E.J., *The Costs of Economic Growth*, (first published 1967) 2nd edn, London, 1993

Mumford, L., *The City in History*, New York, 1961

—, *The Pentagon of Power*, New York, 1970

Northcote, M., *The Environment and Christian Ethics*, Cambridge, 1996

O'Neil, J., *Five Bodies*, Ithaca and London, 1985

Oxfam Position Paper, December 1996, 'Trade Liberalisation as a Threat to Livelihoods: The Corn Sector in the Philippines'

Oxfam Position Paper, April 1997, 'Poor Country Debt Relief'

Oxfam Position Paper, August 1997, 'Debt Relief for Mozambique'

Oxfam Position Paper, September 1997, 'Growth with Equity: An Agenda for Poverty Reduction'

Oxfam Poverty Report 1995, Oxford, 1995

Packard, V., *The Hidden Persuaders*, Harmondsworth and New York, 1957

Pilger, J., *Hidden Agendas*, London, 1998

Polanyi, K., *The Great Transformation: The Political and Economic Origins of our Time*, (first published 1944) Boston, 1957

Postel, S., *The Last Oasis*, London, 1992

Postman, N., *Amusing Ourselves to Death*, London, 1987

Redclift, M., *Wasted: Counting the Costs of Global Consumption*, London, 1996

Reich, R., *The Next American Frontier*, Harmondsworth, 1983

Robbins, L., *An Essay on the Nature and Significance of Economic Science*, London, 1932

Rowbotham, M., *The Grip of Death: A Study of Modern Money, Debt Slavery and Destructive Economics*, Charlbury, 1998

Rowell, A., *Green Backlash: Global Subversion of the Green Movement*, London and New York, 1996

Schumacher, E., *Small is Beautiful*, London, 1973

Schumpeter, J., *Capitalism, Socialism and Democracy*, London, 1974

Scitovsky, T., *The Joyless Economy*, New York, 1976

Seabrook, J., *What Went Wrong? Why Hasn't Having More Made People Happier?* New York, 1978

Shiva, V., *Staying Alive*, London, 1989

Shklar, J., *The Faces of Injustice*, London and New Haven, 1990

Simon, J., *The Ultimate Resource*, Princeton, 1981

Singer, H., and J. Ansari, *Rich and Poor Countries*, 4th edn, London, 1988

Smith, A., *The Wealth of Nations*, (first published 1776) London, 1981

Starke, L., ed., *State of the World 1992*, London, 1992

—, ed., *State of the World 1997*, London, 1997

—, ed., *State of the World 1998*, London, 1998

Thurow, L., *Dangerous Currents: The State of Economics*, New York, 1983

United Nations Human Development Report 1992, Oxford, 1992

United Nations Human Development Report 1997, Oxford, 1997

World Bank Development Report 1992, Oxford, 1992

World Commission on Environment and Development, *Our Common Future*, Oxford, 1987

World Development Movement Briefing, 'A Dangerous Leap in the Dark? Implications of the Multilateral Agreement on Investment', London, 1997

INDEX

INDEX

Keynes, John Maynard, 63, 65
Korea 74
Korten, David, 23, 83, 86–7, 96, 103
Krug, Edward, 53–4
Kyoto summit 45, 55

Lasch, Christopher, 34
Laslett, Peter, 27
limits 23
Lovelock, James, 46

MacIntyre, Alastair, 11, 19–20
Malaysia 57
Mandel, Ernest, 25
Mandeville, Bernard, 30, 31
market 18, 35
Marx, Karl 12–13, 20, 24, 32
Mexico 57, 73, 76, 89
Mishan, E.J., 27, 36, 41, 56
money 23, 85
Mozambique 69, 70
multilateral agreement on investment (MAI)
   83–8
Mumford, Lewis, 9, 23, 33

nation state 103
Newton, John, 20
Niger, Republic of, 69
nuclear energy 58–9

open society 17
Ordine Nuovo 104
Oxfam 49–50, 51, 61, 66–70, 72–74, 84,
   102
ozone layer 53

Packard, Vance, 34
Peru 76
Philippines 37, 57, 70, 74
photosynthesis 48
Pilger, John, 16, 33, 40, 62, 77, 91, 93, 102,
   105–6
planning 83
Plato 16
Polanyi, Karl, 13, 17, 25, 30, 77–8, 85
pollution 41–2, 55, 59
population 41, 47, 97
Postman, Neil, 36
poverty 33, 39, 76
profit 25, 80

radiation 53
recycling 95
Redclift, Michael, 22, 57, 59

Rio summit 84, 98
Robbins, Lionel, 44
Georgescu-Roegen, Nicholas, 46
Rowell, Andrew, 52, 89, 90

Schumacher, E. Fritz, 44
Schumpeter, Joseph, 25, 28
Seabrook, Jeremy, 32
Shiva, Vandana, 26
Shklar, Judith, 88
Smith, Adam, 24, 31, 71
socialism 102–3
Soddy, Frederick, 64
Soros, George, 85, 100
South (Third World) 29, 61–76
South Africa 71
spirituality 93–4
stockmarkets 86
subsidiarity 103–4
sustainable development 45–6, 58, 60–1,
   74–5, 78, 92, 96–7, 105

Tanzania 69
taxes 99, 100
technical fix 94–6
television 75–6
Thailand 37, 57
Thurow, Lester, 68
Tiger economies 62
tourism 37
trade 71–6, 80, 100
transnational corporations (TNCs) 79–80,
   82, 84
transport 98

Uganda 67
United Nations agencies 19, 20, 62, 99,
   100
Uttley, Alison, 38

values 43–4
Venezuela 57
Vietnam 71

wages 87
waste 59
water 48–9
Weber, Max, 60
work conditions 81
World Development Movement 83
Worldwatch Institute 47, 50, 56, 95, 97

Zaire 57
Zimbabwe 69, 70